The hm Learning and Study Skills Program

Teacher's Guide Level 1

Fourth Edition

Edited by Judy Tilton Brunner and Matthew S. Hudson, EdD

ROWMAN & LITTLEFIELD

Lanham • Boulder • New York • London

Published by Rowman & Littlefield
A wholly owned subsidiary of The Rowman & Littlefield Publishing Group, Inc.
4501 Forbes Boulevard, Suite 200, Lanham, Maryland 20706
www.rowman.com

16 Carlisle Street, London W1D 3BT, United Kingdom

British Library Cataloguing in Publication Information Available

Library of Congress Cataloging-in-Publication Data Available
978-1-4758-0386-0 (pbk: alk. paper)—978-1-4758-0387-7 (electronic)

∞™ The paper used in this publication meets the minimum requirements of American National Standard for Information Sciences—Permanence of Paper for Printed Library Materials, ANSI/NISO Z39.48-1992.

Printed in the United States of America

CONTENTS

Introduction to the *hm* Learning and Study Skills Program: Level I I

UNITS

    I. Ways to Listen 15

    II. Tuning into Directions 25

    III. Getting the Timing Down 33

    IV. A Matter of Time 45

    V. Putting Ideas Together 55

    VI. Picturing in Your Mind's Eye 61

    VII. Improving Your Memory 73

    VIII. Organizing Ideas 85

    IX. Reading for Meaning 97

    X. Reading Online and Using Online Texts 111

    XI. Using a Dictionary 119

    XII. Improving Your Vocabulary 129

    XIII. Taking Notes—Mapping and Outlining 137

    XIV. Listening and Taking Notes 151

    XV. Putting a Book Together/Text Features 159

    XVI. Studying and Test Taking 177

    XVII. Multimedia Presentations 191

    XVIII. Posttest 197

INTRODUCTION TO THE *hm* LEARNING AND STUDY SKILLS PROGRAM: LEVEL I

Dear Colleague:

The hm Learning and Study Skills Program: Level I is designed to provide a valuable resource for the teaching of learning and study skills. Please read this introduction carefully to gain a sense of the purposes and values, the means and ends, and the capacities and limitations of this program.

Please note that this is the fourth edition of *The hm Learning and Study Skills Program: Level I.*

Learning and Study Skills: What Are They?

Learning and study skills are methods for acquiring knowledge, understanding, and competence. A look at the listing of units in this program will give examples of important learning and study skills, such as listening, taking notes, and organizing ideas.

In the literal sense, study skills involve specific, observable behaviors that can be described and measured. For example, can a student attend to a set of directions and follow them accurately? Can a student plan the use of his or her study time and follow that schedule? Can a student take useful notes from an oral presentation? Can a student read a section of text and identify the main ideas and important details?

There is also a more profound definition of learning and study skills than this literal one. In this larger sense, learning and study skills are processes for learning. They are processes that help students organize and direct the effort they invest in learning, and their use results in students becoming more effective and efficient learners who are more in charge of their own learning. When students master a skill for learning, they are learning more than just a technique. They are learning a way of solving learning problems, a method of approach and follow-through that can be used in any relevant context. They are also learning more about how to learn effectively. It is this larger understanding of study skills that reveals their central role in schooling.

Learning Skills and Study Skills: What's the Difference?

Many educators equate the terms *learning skills* and *study skills*. Others see a shade of difference in their meanings, with study skills referring primarily to school-based learning and learning skills referring to learning in any context. In this edition of *The hm Learning and Study Skills Program: Level I*, these terms are used interchangeably to emphasize the belief that the skills for learning are essential in every learning context: in school, at home, in post-secondary education, and in the workplace.

As schools meet the needs of students in the twenty-first century, educators must understand students must be active, meaning-seeking and meaning-making learners. Learning and study skills are among the tools students need to be able to use well as they engage in their meaning-seeking and meaning-making activities.

The *hm* Learning and Study Skills Program: Level I

The hm Learning and Study Skills Program: Level I is designed to provide *an introduction to learning and study skills* for fifth-, sixth-, and seventh-grade students through a series of activity-oriented units. Some of the units can be completed in one period of class time. Others will require more than a single period.

The *hm* program is structured on the assumption that activity-oriented lessons are the most effective instructional strategy for the teaching of learning and study skills: more succinctly, that "learning by doing" is the best way to master learning and study skills.

The hm Learning and Study Skills Program: Level I is *not* remedial. Rather, it is designed to assist students at most levels of competence in their development of essential learning and study skills and to reinforce already-existing skills.

The program is deliberately designed to address a wide range of student needs:

1. For the student who has little sense of a particular skill, it provides an introduction to the skill.

2. For the student who is ready to acquire initial competence in a skill, it provides a learning experience.

3. For the student who has already mastered a skill, participation in one of the program's lessons offers review, reinforcement, and the opportunity to increase one's level of competence in that skill.

Thus, the program allows for the participation of students with a wide range of skills and promotes learning on various levels of competence.

The hm Learning and Study Skills Program: Level I can serve as a workbook for classroom use. After the completion of the last unit, it is recommended students keep their workbooks to be a resource and handbook to which they can refer throughout the same school year and subsequent ones. Or, workbooks may be reused as needed.

The Developmental Character of *The hm Learning and Study Skills Program: Level I*

The hm Learning and Study Skills Program: Level I is based on a developmental understanding of the capacities and needs of fifth, sixth, and seventh graders. Young people of these ages still learn effectively through interaction with materials, but many of them are also beginning to develop the capacity for abstraction.

Some of these skills introduced help students use their capacities to listen, visualize, and focus their attention more effectively. Other learning and study skills help young people develop competence in more analytic and abstract areas such as following directions, sequencing, note taking, reading for meaning, and studying.

Study Skills and Learning Preferences

Most individuals have learning preferences. Consequently, learning and study skills should not be taught in a rigid and prescriptive manner that indicates to students that all individuals develop exactly the same repertoire of skills. Rather, as is appropriate to their level of maturity, students need to become metacognitively aware of their own learning preferences. Instruction that is guided by an awareness of individual preferences will help students to develop skills that are specifically useful to their capacities, needs, and desires.

Using *The hm Learning and Study Skills Program: Level I*

When to Teach the *hm* Learning and Study Skills Program: Level I

Classroom use of the *hm* program: level I has demonstrated that the activities in this program are appropriate for fifth, sixth, and seventh graders.

You may also find the program to be of value with some students who are in classes below fifth or above seventh grade.

Where to Teach the *hm* Learning and Study Skills Program

The learning and study skills included in *The hm Learning and Study Skills Program: Level I* are ones that are useful in the study of almost every subject. Thus, the program can be successfully taught within the context of most subjects.

Building Learning and Study Skills Instruction into the Curriculum

It is recommended the units be taught within the context of an already-existing course or class rather than in a mini-course or homeroom setting. Only in the regular classroom can the teacher of the *hm* program integrate study skills with the curriculum of her or his course and help the student to see both the immediate and long-term value of mastering and employing study skills.

If school personnel believe the best place for this content is in an advisory or homeroom setting, or even in a separate study skills class, care should be taken to connect the program information across the curriculum to specific course content. Be aware that each unit offers an introduction to the learning and study skill(s) to be studied and practiced. Most students will need to study and practice each skill(s) over time to achieve competence in using the skill(s).

Pacing of the *hm* Program

There is no recommended single pacing for the teaching of the units. Rather, teachers must decide for themselves how to pace these units in a way that helps students to learn and begin to master the various study skills.

Suggestions for Pacing

a. A division of the instructional responsibility for the units in the program among different subject area teachers, with each one teaching some part of the program;

    b. Three or four units in a one-month period, then, a second month for ongoing practice of these skills, followed by the use of another three or four units in a one-month period, and so on;

    c. One unit every 3–4 weeks over the length of most of the school year;

    d. A focus on 4–6 of these learning and study skills in fifth grade, another 4-6 in sixth grade, and the remaining learning and study skills in seventh grade.

Adopt an instructional strategy for learning and study skills that is suited to the needs of students. Design a strategy that will provide opportunity for the immediate application and reinforcement of the various learning and study skills students can learn through this program.

Preparing Students

Students will approach a unit with more direction, confidence, and enthusiasm if they are given an overview of what will be learned. Find one or two key ideas in the unit introduction of the teacher's guide or use the information from the unit summaries.

Student Discussion

Students need the opportunity to discuss their work if they are to learn study and learning skills effectively and know how and when to use them. Their discussion must include not only the "right answer" (if there is one) but also the process through which they arrived at the answer and their reasons for considering it correct. At this point in a student's development of learning and study skills, *the process is as important as the individual answer*. Oral activities and the opportunity for small- and large-group discussion are part of the lesson design.

Student Perceptions and Expectations

Sometimes students perceive new learning and study skills as more time consuming than their unskilled learning behaviors. In a few cases, this is an accurate perception. Most often, it is not.

Help students gain a wider perspective about their own learning by telling them that any skill, by its very nature, takes more time to use when first learning how to do it. Ask students to think of examples of this from their own experiences. Alternatively, give them a few examples that will illustrate this relationship between competence and time.

College and Career Readiness

With accountability at an all-time high, everyone is concerned about educational outcomes. From the business person who worries about an ill-prepared workforce, to the teacher trying to support students as they read challenging and complex text, to the parents worrying about grades, college admittance, and standardized test scores, everyone understands that college and career readiness must be an attainable goal for all students.

The students of today are living in the fast-paced world of the Internet, YouTube, Google, and smart phones. Educators have made some adjustments, but not nearly as many as will be necessary to make in the next few years.

As some argue for the use of fewer pre-reading strategies, others insist that without the appropriate scaffolding of information, student comprehension will plummet. Regardless, it makes sense for teachers to provide a balanced approach to teaching and learning—supporting when necessary while always working toward the goal of academic independence for all students.

Using the *hm* Learning and Study Skills Program: Pretest, Suggested Directions, Additional Directions, and Unit Summaries

Pre- and Posttesting

Begin by administering the pretest to all students. It is located at the conclusion of the introduction in the teacher and student edition. The purpose of the test is to activate prior knowledge of students as well as to help teachers understand what students know and do not know related to studying effectively. The pretest should not be used as a grade; it should be utilized to begin a serious discussion related to what works and does not work when learning challenging and complex information. Remember, an important part of the discussion is not whether questions are *true* or *false*. Rather, students need to understand *why* something is *true* or *false*. By understanding *why*, they will be more likely to make adjustments in their current study-skill regimen in the hopes of improving grades and learning.

At the conclusion of the program, administer the posttest to all students. It is identical to the pretest (which will help with evaluating learning growth). The student posttest is located in the final section of the student and teacher text.

Suggested Directions

The teacher's guide offers "suggested directions" for the teaching of each unit in the program. The program offers content where students may practice the various skills; however, the teacher may wish to substitute the content of a course in its place if desirable.

Additional Suggestions

Additional teaching suggestions are provided in each unit. These are supplemental teaching activities to be used as reinforcement and additional practice or for the purpose of enriching the unit content. Additional suggestions are indicated by a shaded box

Unit Summaries

Each unit includes a summary. These unit summaries are included both in the student text and in the teacher's guide. Teachers should discuss the information and use the summaries as part of the lesson closure.

Suggested Retrieval Activities

Each unit includes a list of suggested retrieval activities. When completing a unit, these suggestions for closure are meant to further a student's understanding of the material by applying new or enhanced study skills to additional related work. The suggested retrieval activities scaffold a student's learning by using the study skills he or she has listened to, read about, and completed exercises on, to applying that information learned in context. This application provides the highest level of learning for the student.

Technology Adaptation

The suggested uses for technology have been included for two primary reasons. First, technology is appealing to students and teachers; it sparks an interest when the learner might otherwise disengage. Secondly, the use of online resources adds a dimension to learning both vast and global. While none of the lessons within this series *requires* the use of technology, many can be *enhanced* using websites and other resources. Teachers should be familiar with www .classroom20.com and www.cybraryman.com. These invaluable resources provide new and innovative programs for classroom use. When possible, teachers should use all of the technological resources available within the school. If students are truly to be college and career ready, the appropriate use of technology must be part of each day's lessons. However, because many schools have limited technological assets, all lessons can be implemented without the use of an electronic component.

The challenge for educators will be enhancing their own knowledge related to technology while maintaining a commitment to innovative and engaging instructional strategies. Specific web-related resources are included in the multimedia presentations unit.

Teacher's Guide Notes

This teacher's guide includes exact copies of the student text and how it appears in each unit. This allows the teacher to have detailed notes and instructions, while also being able to see what the students have in front of them. The student text is identified by a box and smaller text size. Answers are provided in italics when appropriate. The introduction to the program as it appears in the student edition is located at the end of this section.

Suggestions and Recommendations

Using Small Groups in the Classroom

For several units in the *hm* program, the use of small, cooperative groups of students working on the various exercises is recommended for the following reasons:

a. The interactions within small groups of students working on a common task can facilitate the learning of skills through shared problem solving. In this way, students can share their talents and experience and learn from each other.

b. Small-group processes offer a superb method of genuinely engaging students in an activity. Such processes help both to enhance motivation for learning and to increase interest in the content of a lesson, because they offer active participation to each student.

c. Membership of small groups should be based on the teacher's knowledge of students. Sometimes it works best if groups are heterogeneous. Other times homogeneous groups may work better. Regardless of the type of grouping, students need both individual and group accountability.

Individual work is of critical importance to the learning of study skills. When a skill is introduced in a group setting, it becomes crucial to provide for individual work with that skill through homework and/or other class activities.

Learning Study Skills: Trial and Error

People learn skills through processes of repeated trial and error. One key to learning- and study-skills teaching, then, is providing students with sufficient opportunity for practicing the skill to be learned. *The hm Learning and Study Skills Program: Level I* includes only a few practices of each skill it introduces. If students are to master the learning and study skills presented by the program, it is essential they be provided with structured and ongoing opportunities for practice of the various skills. For example, some teachers have selected four or five learning and study skills that they judged to be of the greatest value in their classes and have focused their instruction on these in the weeks and months after their initial use of the entire program.

Of course, there is an inevitable tension between providing students with trial-and-error practice of a new learning skill and helping students maintain their interest in mastering the skill in the face of the necessary repetition. While this tension cannot be willed away, it can be minimized through the use of variation and imagination in the instructional design. For example, if students are learning to take notes, let them practice their skills in a wide variety of contexts and for many different purposes. Also, as students practice a new learning and study skill, help them to see the benefits they will gain from their increasing mastery of the skill.

Learning Study Skills: Learning from Errors

An important key to teaching learning and study skills is the recognition that learning a new skill requires most learners to err before they can succeed. Students learn skills by being presented with a new skill, trying to use that skill, committing errors, identifying errors, and correcting them. Understanding this process creates several responsibilities for the teacher:

a. The teacher must encourage students to ask questions when they do not understand an idea or directive. Knowing when to ask questions is an important characteristic of the effective learner.

b. The teacher must provide a space within the learning process where students can try out a new skill, make errors, but not feel that they have failed or are "failures."

c. The teacher must provide students with enough opportunities for practice of the new skill so that students begin to master the skill and see its usefulness.

d. The teacher must provide usable feedback to students about the effectiveness of their use of the new learning skill they understand that they can now do certain things they could not do before.

e. The teacher must reward students for what they have done well in using the new skill. With such recognition, students experience success in the learning process, validated both by their own new ability and by the teacher's recognition of this. The experience of success motivates students to continue the development of mastery of the new learning skill.

Grading and the *hm* Learning and Study Skills Program

Given the grade-oriented reality of most schools, students' involvement with the *hm* program may be graded in some fair and concrete manner. A standards-based approach for grading is recommended. With standards-based grading, students' grades result not from each practice with the skill but from the level of competence students achieve with the skill at the end of a certain amount of time.

Prior to beginning the program, students should understand how their work with the *hm* program will be evaluated.

Additional Comments

The *hm* Learning and Study Skills Program is designed to be taught by a teacher in a classroom setting. It is not programmed material students can work through by themselves, although some of the units can be used on an individual basis.

The *hm* Learning and Study Skills Program incorporates as much student activity as possible, including individual, small-group, and whole-class activities. This emphasis results from a belief that people learn study skills best by practicing.

It's important to note that the *hm* program can also serve as a diagnostic tool. An inspection of student work in various units will provide specific information about their learning- and study-skills competencies. It will show what they already know and what needs additional instructional attention.

It is best to provide students with an overview concerning the values and purposes of learning and study skills both in the classroom and throughout their lives.

Other *hm* Learning and Study Skills Programs

The *hm* Learning and Study Skills Programs include the following:

The *hm* Study Skills Program: Level A—for grades 1–2

The *hm* Study Skills Program: Level B—for grades 3–4

The *hm* Learning and Study Skills Program: Level I—for grades 5–7

The *hm* Learning and Study Skills Program: Level II—for grades 8–10

The *hm* Learning and Study Skills Program: Level III—for grades 11–13

The *hm* Math Learning and Study Skills Program—for grades 6–10

The *hm* Science Learning and Study Skills Program—for grades 7–10

The *hm* Study Skills Program Inventory 1—for grades 4–7

The *hm* Study Skills Program Inventory 2—for grades 8–12

Parents' Guide to Learning and Study Skills

Pretest and Posttest

Suggested Directions for the Study Skills Pretest

1. Talk with students about the importance of being organized and the value of a routine for studying.

2. Read out loud the directions for the survey and make sure students understand there is no right or wrong answer. Rather, the most important thing is for them to be honest in what they do and don't do.

3. After students have completed the assignment, discuss the reasons why each statement is relevant to good study habits. The reasons in the teacher's edition are in italics.

Suggested Directions for the Study Skills Posttest

1. Explain to students that the purpose of the posttest is to measure what has been learned from using *The hm Learning and Study Skills Program: Level I.*

2. In addition to marking "Always," "Sometimes," or "Never," students should include an explanation as to why there might be a difference between what they actually do and what they should be doing.

Study Skills Survey

	Always	Sometimes	Never
I review my assignments every day. *The more frequent the review of daily lessons, the easier it is to recall the information on test day. Frequent review supports long-term retention.*			
I try to study in a quiet place. *Although some students believe they can do several things at one time, this is not true for learning. The human brain can only concentrate on one thing at a time.*			
When necessary, I ask for help. *Students need to use the resources available to them. This can be parents, classmates, or teachers.*			
I keep a folder for each subject. *A key to staying organized is making sure that each subject has its own folder and place to keep handouts and assignments.*			
I keep my folders organized. *Middle school students are notorious for not keeping folders organized. However, they usually respond positively to reminders.*			
I write sample test questions and answer the questions. *Part of preparing for an exam is anticipating what might be asked. Students should get in the habit of writing sample test questions and answers as part of the reviewing process.*			
I do my homework as early in the day as possible. *Students are busy people, too. If they wait too long after school to begin completing homework, it will not be good. The later in the evening, the more tired the student becomes. The more tired the student, the less productive in terms of learning.*			
I keep a "to-do" list of assignments. *A good habit to develop at an early age is keeping a "to-do" list. For students this would include homework assignments, due dates, extracurricular schedules, etc.*			
I turn in all assignments on time. *Procrastination works against most people. Most teachers are unwilling to give full credit to students that turn in assignments late. Students should understand it is foolish to lose points because of tardiness.*			
When I take notes, I always write a summary from my notes of what I learned. *Reviewing and writing a summary of notes taken from a book, a class discussion, or a class lecture helps to cement the information into long-term memory.*			
I begin studying for tests several days in advance of the exam. *Last-minute test preparation is not a good habit. Learning in small increments is much more efficient, and it also helps to eliminate test anxiety.*			

	Always	Sometimes	Never
I compare my notes to a classmate's notes. *Comparing notes with a classmate can help both students. It can ensure that notes are complete and comprehensive.*			
I take written notes over text material. *When a reading assignment is made, students should assume the teacher believes the information is important enough to warrant note taking. This usually means the information will appear on an upcoming test.*			
I look at bold print, italics, the writing in margins, and study questions before I begin a reading assignment. *Using the features of a text is a good studying strategy. The author and publisher usually designate what is the most important content to be learned.*			
I ask the teacher to explain things when I'm confused. *It is surprising how few students will stop a teacher and ask for further explanation. This may be a fear of believing he or she is the only one that is unsure. Regardless, students should be encouraged to ask when something is unclear.*			
When learning new information, I read the text slowly. *Good readers know that different tasks require different rates of reading. As a result, adjustments to reading rates should be made depending on familiarity of content and purpose for reading.*			
When I have several homework assignments, I finish the hardest ones first. *There is a feeling of satisfaction when a difficult task is completed. If the more challenging assignment is "saved for later," fatigue sets in and it makes it even more difficult to complete.*			
When I sit down to study, I have all my supplies organized and ready to use— paper, pencils, computer, etc. *Organization is important, and students should designate a specific place for studying each day. Students can waste several minutes of a studying time by repeatedly trying to find supplies.*			

STUDENT TEXT

Introduction to Learning and Study Skills

How Do You Learn?

Not everyone learns in the same way. Some people like to read about something new before they try it. Other people like to learn when they can actually "do" whatever they are learning. Some want to be able to imagine how to do something before they try it. Still others like to be told about a new thing. They like to discuss it before they try to do it. Can you think of any other ways that people learn to do new things?

What is your preference?

STUDENT TEXT

Exercise I

Directions: What do you do well? Look at the list below, and pick *one* thing that you feel you have learned to do well. Or if you prefer, pick your own activity. Write your choice on the space provided. Be sure to pick something you remember learning.

read	cook	debate
write	play a sport	use a word processor
sail	ride a bike	play a computer game
ski	find Internet information	knit
play an instrument	draw	care for an animal
sew	ice-skate	solve math problems

Exercise II

Directions: Think about the thing you learned to do very well. How did you learn to do it?

watching	listening	doing
reading	thinking about	working when I have to
experimenting	writing	getting it right
learning from my mistakes	proving my point	"hands on"
being creative	talking it over	with a group
with a friend	by myself	asking questions
doing something I care about	looking things up	get a feeling that it's right
practice		

Look at the words and phrases listed. Circle the ones that describe how you learn best. You may also write other words and phrases that describe how you learn in the space provided.

_____

_____

_____

_____

_____

Remember: There are no right or wrong answers! You can circle and write as many words and phrases as you need to describe how you learn.

(*continued*)

Exercise III

Directions: Look again at the list in Exercise I. This time pick out something that you have had *trouble* trying to learn well. Or if you prefer, pick your own activity. Write your choice on the space provided.

_____

_____

_____

1. How did you try to learn the thing you said you had *trouble* learning? Look at the list in Exercise II again. Pick some ways that you tried to learn, and write these ways in the space provided.

_____

_____

_____

_____

_____

2. Have you chosen any different ways than you chose for Exercise II?

_____

If you answered "yes," write the different ways in the space provided.

_____

_____

_____

_____

_____

What Are Learning and Study Skills?

Learning and study skills are *ways or methods for learning*. They are ways of doing what you are asked to do in school that can help you to learn better. When you use learning and study skills, you can often get more done in a given period of time and learn more, too.

Some examples of learning and study skills are these: active listening, tuning into directions, reading for meaning, taking notes, solving problems, and preparing for tests.

How Do You Learn Study and Learning Skills?

People learn study and learning skills through practice. You don't learn how to play basketball or use a keyboard by talking about it. You have to play it. The same is true with learning and study skills.

(continued)

13

You often learn study and learning skills best through the mistakes you make. Everyone makes mistakes. What's important is that you look at your mistakes carefully and find out what caused them. When you know what caused a particular mistake, you'll know how not to make that mistake again.

Why Are Learning and Study Skills Important?

Learning will not suddenly become simple just because you have learned to use learning and study skills. But these skills will help you to become a better learner. You will probably find school more rewarding and enjoyable. You will also be more able to learn whatever you want outside of school.

Directions for the Study Skills Pretest

Before beginning this program, complete the survey that follows. Be honest with your answers.

Study Skills Survey

	Always	Sometimes	Never
I review my assignments every day.			
I try to study in a quiet place.			
When necessary, I ask for help.			
I keep a folder for each subject.			
I keep my folders organized.			
I write sample test questions and answer the questions.			
I do my homework as early in the day as possible.			
I keep a "to-do" list of assignments.			
I turn in all assignments on time.			
When I take notes, I always write a summary from my notes of what I learned.			
I begin studying for tests several days in advance of the exam.			
I compare my notes to a classmate's notes.			
I take written notes over text material.			
I look at bold print, italics, the writing in margins, and study questions before I begin a reading assignment.			
I ask the teacher to explain things when I'm confused.			
When learning new information, I read the text slowly.			
When I have several homework assignments, I finish the hardest ones first.			
When I sit down to study, I have all my supplies organized and ready to use—paper, pencils, computer, etc.			

UNIT I
WAYS TO LISTEN

Listening skills are often overlooked during the middle school years, yet these skills are crucial to the achievement of academic success.

This unit provides the students with a learning experience about the effectiveness of their own listening skills. It also gives them a procedure in "Steps in Active Listening" that they can use to improve their listening skills.

In addition, the unit provides an instrument to gain a sense of (1) how well students listen to the teacher and (2) how well students listen to each other. It also offers a way to include the steps in active listening in other areas of the curriculum.

Suggested Directions for Unit I

Please note: This unit usually requires two class periods.

Class Period I

1. Two different ways of organizing the central activity of this unit, "Ways to Listen," are offered. Read through both sets of directions, and select the method most appropriate for the class.

First Alternative

1. Before teaching this lesson, read each situation, and make one copy of each one on a separate piece of paper. (All situations are included in this unit.)

2. At the beginning of the period, divide the class into small groups of 4–6 students.

STUDENT TEXT

Listening Is More Than Just Hearing

The average student spends more than half of each school day *listening*. That means that you give more time to listening than to anything else you do in school.

Most people think of listening as something as natural as walking or eating. They don't think of it as anything you have to work at to do well. But we are not *born* good listeners. We learn to be good listeners.

Why is this so? Hearing is a natural ability, but *listening* is more than just hearing. Listening means directing your attention to—or *focusing on*—what you're hearing and trying to make sense of what you've heard.

Listening is a study skill. It's one of the most important study skills because listening is a part of almost everything else that you do. It seems simple, but it's not. Being a good listener doesn't come naturally. It requires learning and practice.

Why Is It Hard to Listen Even When Interested?

Generally people talk at a rate of about 125 words per minute. However, we think at a speed that is more than three times as fast, about 400 words per minute. That means our thoughts move much faster than the words we hear. So it's not surprising that we often let our attention wander away from what another person is saying to us.

The key to becoming a good listener is to be an *active* listener: to keep your thoughts *focused* on what is heard.

---

3. Read aloud "Listening Is More Than Just Hearing" and "Why Is It Hard to Listen Even When Interested?" Discuss briefly. Then read the directions to "The Listening Game" aloud to the class. Select one student in each group to be a *reader*. Ask the members of the class who are not *readers* to answer the question in "Try It Again: The Listening Game." While they are doing this, gather the *readers* together. Hand a different *situation* to each group *reader*. Explain to the readers they will have to do the following tasks:

   a. Read the *situation* aloud to the group only once. Read slowly and clearly. Do not repeat anything. Also, do not answer any questions.

   b. When finished reading, stay with the group. Listen to the discussion, but do not participate in it. Remember as much as possible. Be prepared to tell the class what was said.

   c. Repeat the process so more than one student has the opportunity to be reporters and readers.

STUDENT TEXT

The Listening Game

Directions: A story will be read aloud to you only *once*. Pay close attention to the details of the story. When the story is finished, you will be asked to tell what you have heard. Listen carefully! (You are not allowed to take notes.)

---

4. Read the original version of that situation aloud. Ask students to suggest one or two ways in which the *situation* has been changed. List these on the board. Repeat the same process with the other *reporters* and *situations*. Then discuss the ways in which the situations changed through the listening process.

Second Alternative

1. Before class, make enough copies of situation B for half your class; do the same with situation C.

2. Read aloud "Listening Is More Than Just Hearing" and "Why Is It Hard to Listen Even When Interested?" Then read the directions to "The Listening Game" aloud to the class. Then read situation A aloud. Have two or three students give their version of what they have heard. Then read the original situation again, and discuss how the situation is changed through the listening process.

3. Divide the class into pairs. Pass out situation B to one member of each pair, and situation C to the other member. Have the students with situation B read it aloud to their partners. Then have the listeners tell the readers what they have heard. Ask a student to read situation B aloud to the class. Then discuss the students' experience of how the situation was changed through the listening process.

4. Repeat the same process with situation C, having the students reverse roles.

Class Period 2

Use the same teaching format used for "The Listening Game." Prepare your own context paragraphs for this activity. Students will benefit the most if the paragraphs relate directly to something they are currently learning. Workbooks, textbooks, and references can provide resources for appropriate paragraphs.

Make sure that the paragraphs have a clearly stated main idea and several related details. It is also important for the content of the paragraphs to be about a topic the students can visualize.

STUDENT TEXT

Steps in Active Listening

It is a *fact* that we can all become active listeners. So remember the word *fact*. It will help you remember the steps in *active listening*, because the first letter of each of the steps spells the word *FACT*.

Step 1: <u>F</u>ocus

The first step in active listening is to *focus*. This means to give your attention to something. Television often "catches" your attention. It doesn't require you to do the active work of *focusing*. However, when your father calls you from the next room as you are watching television, you have to pull your mind from the television to really focus on what he is saying.

(continued)

Step 2: Ask

While you listen, *ask* yourself questions about what the speaker is saying. Then try to answer your questions, or see if the speaker answers them. Asking and answering questions in this way can help you make sense of the speaker's message.

When you are listening in school, you might *ask* yourself: What is it that the teacher wants me to know? Do I understand this? What don't I understand about what I am hearing? Does this make sense to me?

Step 3: Connect

Keep asking yourself why the speaker is saying what she or he is saying. Try to *connect* the main ideas with each other. For instance, the speaker may talk about growing food in a certain place. You already know that these things are needed for people to grow food: climate, soil conditions, and technology. As the speaker is talking, you will listen for and *connect* the main ideas of climate, soil conditions, and technology in order to understand how the food is grown.

Step 4: Try to Picture

Try to picture in your mind what the speaker is saying. Some people find that they can listen and remember better if they use their imaginations to make *mind pictures*. For example, if you are listening to a set of directions about how to get somewhere, make an imaginary map of the directions in your mind.

1. Read over the "Steps in Active Listening" with students. Discuss each step, and relate it to "The Listening Game" that the students played the previous day.

STUDENT TEXT

Try It Again: The Listening Game

Directions: Again a story will be read to you only *once*. Try out the *steps in active listening*. *Focus* on the speaker so you can pay close attention to the details of the story. *Ask* yourself how these details *connect*. *Try to picture* what is happening.

When the story is finished, you will be asked to tell what you have heard.

1. Did you find listening any easier this time? _____ If so, why?

   _____

   _____

   _____

   _____

2. Which of the *steps in active listening* is the most difficult for you to do?

   _____

   _____

   _____

   _____

(continued)

18

3. Why do you think this is so?

_____

_____

_____

_____

2. Repeat the procedure used for "The Listening Game" during day 1 with "Try It Again: The Listening Game," but use your own paragraphs.

3. Have the students answer questions 1 and 2 when they finish "Try It Again: The Listening Game." When they have done so, discuss the students' answers to the questions.

4. Read over the *summary*. Highlight the steps in active listening. Explain to the students how they can use the acronym *FACT* to help them remember the four steps.

The directions for these situations give the teacher an option to distribute copies of the material. To make that easier for the teacher, we suggest formatting the pagination where each situation may be easily copied and not continue over 2 pages.

Situation A

We are all witnesses to an automobile accident. Listen carefully as I read to you what we have all "seen."

We were all standing at the intersection of South Street and East Avenue in Springfield, Missouri. It was late in the morning. A blue sedan, carrying only a driver, slowed, signaled, and made a right turn from South Street onto East Avenue without bothering to obey the stop sign.

The truck racing up East Avenue caught the side of the sedan's rear bumper. The sedan spun into a fire hydrant, breaking the hydrant in two. A flow of water came rushing out from the hydrant stump, and the neighborhood children were soon splashing in the water on this hot July day.

Situation B

We are all witnesses to a bank robbery. Listen carefully as I read to you what we all have "seen."

At 1:00 p.m. we were standing in the lobby of the Bank of Canada in Edmonton, Alberta. Three persons dressed in clown outfits with faces painted white skipped into the bank. Each wore the same costume, except that one had a red hat, another a green one, and the third a yellow one.

The clown with the red hat went to the teller at the last window while the other two clowns juggled oranges in the middle of the bank. Then the clown with the yellow hat began to shout advertisements for the circus. The clown with the green hat went from person to person selling tickets until the bank manager came out to chase the two of them away. By the time he got both clowns out through the revolving doors, the clown in the red hat had also disappeared.

A minute later the bank manager walked to the last window. He found that the teller had fainted and that $5,000 was missing from the drawer.

Situation C

We are all witnesses to a rescue on the beach. Listen carefully as I read to you what we have all "seen."

We were all standing on the edge of the beach on Pelican Lake, which is located just outside Silver Springs, Georgia. It was just after noon because we had heard the noon bell from the fire station only a few minutes before.

A boy of about ten years was fishing from a rowboat. His line jerked fiercely, and he stood up to reel in what might be a big catch. As he started to pull it in, a motorboat towing a water-skier roared by. The skier's wake rolled up against the rowboat and knocked the boy into the water.

A big labrador retriever swam out into the lake and grabbed the boy by the collar of his shirt. Both boy and dog made it safely back to shore, and the motorboat vanished around the bend in the lake.

Situation D

We are all witnesses to a tornado. Listen carefully as I read to you what we all have "seen."

It was August 29th, a very hot and humid day in Wellcove, Texas. We were sitting on the front porch of our house trying to cool off. It was already late in the afternoon when we noticed the sky turning a bright yellow. A few minutes later we saw funnel-shaped clouds coming in from the west.

We knew that they were tornado clouds, so we ran into the basement for safety. Through the basement window, we saw a pickup truck lifted up by the wind and set down on the top of a downtown department store. On the other side of our street, all the windows were broken.

Later we found out that some of the stores such as the hardware store also had their insides knocked out. But others weren't damaged much at all. In the ice cream parlor, the cones were stacked in neat piles on the counter just behind the broken windows. On our side of the street, nothing was touched at all, except for a barber pole that was knocked over.

Situation E

We are all witnesses to a poodle kidnapping. Listen carefully as I read to you what we have all "seen."

It was April 15th, a warm day in San Francisco. We were all waiting in the boarding lounge at the airport. Our jet was scheduled to leave for New York in fifteen minutes.

A gray miniature poodle with pink bows tied on its head was sitting on the lap of a well-dressed woman. Many people had stopped to pat the little dog on the head and ask the woman how it was going to travel aboard the airplane. She was explaining the airline rules and the dog's black carrying case to an elderly man when a firecracker exploded about two feet away. The dog bolted into the crowd.

We saw a man in a gray raincoat pick up the dog and run through the crowd into a room marked "Employees Only." We watched until we had to board the plane. Nobody entered or left the room.

Situation F

We are all witnesses to a window cleaner's accident. Listen carefully as I read to you what we all have "seen."

It was early in the morning of September 9, a bright and warm day. We had just arrived at work on the top floor of the old Crest Building in Baltimore. A few minutes later, we saw the window cleaner appear on the scene. He spent almost an hour setting up pulleys and a platform. Then he was finally ready to step out onto the platform and clean the windows.

About an hour later we saw a huge orange balloon floating past the windows. The balloon was about 60 feet tall. Hanging from the bottom of the balloon was a wicker basket with a young woman standing in it. The basket swung too close to the building and appeared to knock the window cleaner off the platform. We all rushed to the window to see what had happened. The woman in the basket had grabbed the window cleaner. His feet were kicking in mid-air. Finally they glided away from the building and landed safely in a chestnut tree in the middle of the park across the street.

Additional Suggestions

1. Create enjoyable activities that encourage students to listen well. If they feel successful about listening in "game"-type activities, they will also feel positive about listening in other learning activities. Some ways to do this are the following:

   a. Get road map sets for the class. Put students in pairs. Have the partners each decide on a destination. Each student should mark his or her own route in red. Taking turns, the partners give directions to each other on how to follow their created routes. The listeners mark the new route in blue. Afterward they compare routes to see how well they listened.

   b. "The Listening Game" format is a good way to introduce a new unit in science or social studies. Find paragraphs that outline a main idea of the unit and contain several details. Read the paragraphs aloud. Ask the students to restate the main idea and repeat as many details as they can remember.

   c. Use the same kind of motivation taught by games in a classroom teaching. For example, when doing a science experiment, say, "We're going to prove air takes up space. Maybe you could show your parents the same experiment tonight and explain to them what you have learned."

2. Effective listening skills are often closely related to the child's ability to visualize what he or she is hearing. Students learn to visualize more effectively by providing them with practice in listening *and* visualizing. For example, read a description of the eye or the heart and ask the students to draw or diagram what they have heard. (Assure students they need not have any skill in drawing.) Or use descriptions of a battle, an imaginary creature, or a kind of food. Or lead students through an imaginary experience of

some physical activity before they conduct the activity physically. Be sure to integrate this kind of exercise into the regular curriculum. Also, be careful to ask students to draw or diagram something that is relatively simple but that requires attention to detail. Use situation A from this unit as an example of how visualizing helps students remember. Review that situation, and draw it on the board or use the overhead projector. Then design a similar situation to read to the class. Have them map it out as you read it.

3. There are three general kinds of listening:

   a. listening for information and organization;

   b. critical listening; and

   c. listening for appreciation and enjoyment.

   Involve students in experiences that are directed to each of these kinds of listening. Explain to your students that there are different ways to listen. For instance, when reading a story to them, ask them to imagine the setting and characters to help them remember the main parts of the story. This is different from trying to remember the sequence to a set of directions. It helps to tell them what type of a listening task they have to do, what they must listen for, and what they will do as a result of listening.

4. Teach students to listen carefully! Try not to repeat instructions. Instead, from the very first day of the school year, accustom the class to the expectation that the teacher will say things only *once*. (This may be a struggle in the beginning, but the rewards for everyone are worth the effort.)

   Explain to students that only clarifying questions will be allowed. If giving a complicated set of directions, explain to the students why directions may need to be repeated for some types of directions—but not for all.

5. Give students the opportunity to use the steps in active listening. Create learning experiences that illustrate each step.

STUDENT TEXT

Unit I Summary

We are not born as good listeners. We have to learn to listen well. Active listening is a study skill.

We can learn to listen actively by following these steps:

Focus: Look at the speaker. Try to pay attention to what is being said.

Ask questions: Try to figure out what is important by asking questions. Then answer your questions, or see if the speaker answers your questions.

Connect: "Make sense" out of what the speaker is saying by *connecting* main ideas with each other.

Try to picture: Try to see "in your mind's eye" what the speaker is talking about.

Suggested Retrieval Activities

As part of closure and retrieval of information learned, ask students to do one or more of the following:

- Write 4 things that could help to improve listening skills.

- Imagine there will be a test for this unit. Prepare a "Cheat Sheet."

STUDENT TEXT

Technology Adaptation

- Listen to a podcast, and write a summary of what was learned.

- Listen to a program on National Public Radio. Take notes during the program and compare the notes to a classmate's notes.

- Listen to a chapter of an audio book. Draw a picture of what was learned.

UNIT II
TUNING INTO DIRECTIONS

By this age, students are well acquainted with many of the standard practices used in the classroom. As a result of this familiarity as well as other factors, they often do not read or listen to directions carefully. Instead they make assumptions about directions based on their previous experience. Even the best students may try to begin an assignment before reading the instructions.

This unit can help students begin to recognize the importance of attending carefully to both oral and written directions. There are two exercises in this unit. The first one focuses the students' awareness on the task of listening to and following directions. The second exercise gives the students an opportunity to sharpen the skills they must use when listening to and following directions.

In Exercise I, the first direction tells the students they will spell a word in pencil or crayon. As the students look at the diagram, many will immediately perceive the word *listen*. Some may go to work at once as a result of this perception, without listening and following the other instructions. As the task progresses, others may tune out the teacher.

The purpose of this exercise is not to trick the students but to help them discover at what point they tune the teacher out and no longer attend to instructions. This activity provides a diagnostic tool in reference to the students' skill in reading and listening to directions and following them. Ask students who got the "wrong answer" if they can discover when and why they "tuned out" the directions.

The second exercise provides a means through which the students can practice whatever went "wrong" in the first exercise. It also gives students an opportunity to experience the difficulty involved in giving clear directions.

STUDENT TEXT

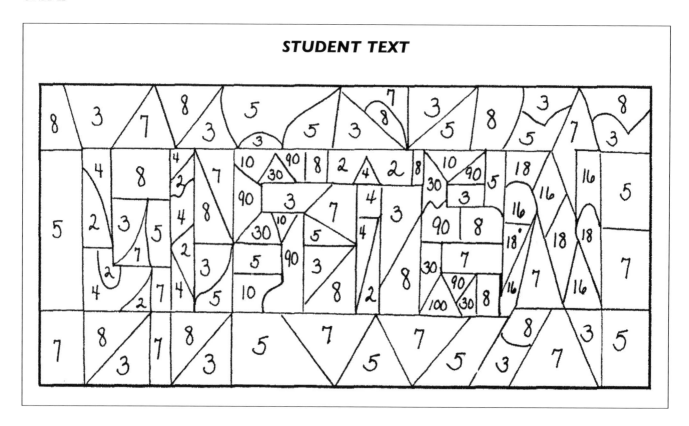

Suggested Directions for Unit II

1. Read all of Exercise I in the Student Text carefully. The last two paragraphs before the unit summary instruct students to follow only directions 3, 7, and 9. If they play the game correctly, they will create the word *lit*. If they play it incorrectly, the word will be *listen*.

2. Make sure each student has a pencil and a crayon.

3. Tell the students they will be playing a game that will show how well they listen to and follow directions.

Read the directions that follow aloud. (These directions begin with "Open your Learning and Study Skills Programs" and conclude with direction 10.) Read slowly and clearly. Be sure to read each number as well as each direction. Pause for about five seconds between directions. The last direction is the most important one, but don't overemphasize it.

Directions to Be Read to Students

Open your Learning and Study Skills Programs to "Tuning into Directions," and we're going to play a game involving following directions. Now turn your books so that the numbers on the diagram are right side up.

I'm going to read a set of directions to you. *Don't do anything* until I have finished reading the whole set of directions. Then I will read them again, but only one more time. Use the first reading as a preview. You will need this reading to keep in tune for the second reading.

i. One clue is that you will end up with a word spelled out in crayon when you are done with this game. Another clue is that there is a trick to the game.

ii. Color in pencil all spaces containing the number seven.

iii. Color in crayon all spaces containing the number two.

iv. Color in crayon all spaces containing multiples of ten. (If your students are not familiar with this concept, you can say all numbers that end in zero instead.)

v. Color in pencil all spaces containing the number eight.

vi. Color in crayon all spaces containing even numbers between eleven and nineteen.

vii. Color in crayon all spaces containing the number four.

viii. Color in pencil all spaces containing the number five and the number three.

ix. Write the word that you have spelled out on the line below the diagram. If you have the correct word, you have won the game!

x. You will not need this direction the second time through, but now it is important. You will find information that you need to win this game in Exercise I. Turn to Exercise I now, and read it carefully. You will have _____ minutes to do this.

*Decide how much time the students will need to read, and tell them they will have that amount of time when you read direction 10.

STUDENT TEXT

Exercise I

You will find that listening to and following directions is a very important skill. This is true not only in schoolwork but also in your daily life. Probably each of you has a story about a time when you only half heard or didn't hear a direction. Afterward you found yourself in a complete mess, like the man in the old joke:

He thought they said "trains" when they passed out brains, so he ran to catch one.

Never got himself a brain!

It seems that the man in the joke shares a problem with many people. Some students in a midwestern school received very poor grades on an achievement test. When they investigated the cause of these results, guidance counselors and classroom teachers found not poor students but poor listeners. These students had never before taken this kind of test. They weren't tuned in to listening to and following directions. So they could only guess at what they were supposed to do.

(continued)

You can't guess about directions and expect to be right! You need to listen carefully and ask questions if you don't understand what you have heard.

You are already showing that you are a good listener because you are reading this page as you were instructed. Now here's an important clue! You must listen to and follow only directions number 3, 7, and 9 the next time your teacher reads the directions.

The students in the midwestern school were then taught how to listen to directions. They also learned to read directions more carefully. When they took the achievement test again, they did much better. After you have read this page carefully, keep the secret to yourself! Write 3, 7, and 9 on the page before this one so you will know what directions to follow. Listen carefully, follow the right directions, and you will spell the right word in crayon.

4. When the students have completed their reading, repeat directions 1–9. Pause about five seconds after giving each direction.

5. Tell the students that the winning word is *lit*. Discuss the importance of following the directions in this game. Engage the students in trying to figure out where they "went wrong" by asking questions such as the following ones:

- When did you think you knew the answer? Why did seeing the word *listen* in the diagram make it difficult for you to follow directions?

- Did you start following the directions on the first reading? Why did you do that? How many felt that the directions were so long and confusing that you had to start right away?

- Did you read carefully?

- Did anyone follow the directions accurately but not believe the word could be something other than "listen"?

- Can you think of any other time when you jumped ahead because you thought you knew what you were doing and got into trouble as a result?

Additional Suggestions

1. Involve the class in playing the game of "Airplane and Pilot." In this game, one student is blindfolded. He is the *airplane*. The classroom is then set up into an obstacle course. Choose a *pilot* to land the *airplane* successfully by giving her or him oral directions. Repeat the game with a new *airplane*, *pilot*, and obstacle course.

2. Cut out identical sets of shapes from sheets of tagboard. Have a set of shapes for each student.

   Organize the class into pairs, with one member of each pair identified as A and the other as B. Have the pairs sit back to back on the floor. Give each student an identical set of shapes.

Have the A's arrange their shapes into a figure design. When they have done so, have each A give directions to her or his partner so that the partner can make an exact copy of the A's design or figure without looking at it.

This activity is especially rich because certain discrepancies in giving directions emerge. Students have to decide if "on top of" looks like this:

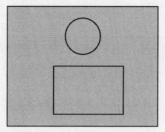

Or like this:

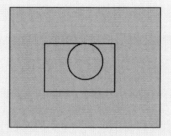

After one attempt and discussion, have the A's and B's switch roles and try again.

You can also have students write out directions for the arrangement of the shapes and see if a partner can follow the written directions.

3. In the beginning of a new school year, it is always fun to play an "Introductions Game." This is an activity that begins by putting the students in a circle.

Choose a student to begin by introducing himself or herself, telling the class one important thing about himself or herself, and leaving an opening for the person on his or her right to introduce himself or herself. For example:

"Hi, my name is Mark. I wonder how I'll like this new school. This is . . ."

The next person must introduce herself or himself as well as all the people who have gone before her or him.

"My name is Carey. Our family just got a new German shepherd. This is Mark. He is wondering if he'll like this school. This is . . ."

Work through the circle until all members of the class are introduced.

4. Select a written passage from any subject area to read to the students. Change certain words or phrases throughout the passage so their meaning becomes nonsensical or irrelevant. Ask the students to listen

and think about the passage as it is read aloud at an even pace. Have the students raise their hands whenever they hear a word that does not make sense. Review the passage orally or on an overhead projector to discuss the changed wording.

5. Create humorous irregularities or insert incorrect ideas in subject matter that students are currently studying. Start out with fairly obvious miscues. Then increase the level of subtlety as the students become more discriminating.

6. As a variation, have the students keep a count on paper during a first reading. Compare the number of "mistakes" that the students heard. Then have the students raise their hands as described above during a second reading of the passage.

STUDENT TEXT

Unit II Summary

Remember the steps in active listening from Unit I. They are these:

Focus: Look at the speaker. Try to pay attention to what is being said.

Ask questions: Try to figure out what is important by asking questions. Then answer your questions, or see if the speaker answers your questions.

Connect: *Make sense* out of what the speaker is saying by *connecting* main ideas with each other.

Try to picture: Try to see *in your mind's eye* what the speaker is saying.

Reading and listening to directions is an important skill. This is true not only in school but in any situation in life.

Always read directions carefully. Be sure to read *all* of the directions. Then if you don't understand, ask questions. If you are not allowed to ask questions, ask yourself the questions and listen for the answers.

Listen carefully when someone is giving you directions. Don't try to guess what they are. Listen to *all* of the directions. Then if you don't understand what you've heard, ask questions.

If you can't remember all the directions, write them down on a piece of paper.

Suggested Retrieval Activities

As part of closure and retrieval of information learned, ask students to do one or more of the following:

- Tell a classmate two things learned that will help with grades and learning.

- Write on a sheet of paper the lesson's learning objective. Explain how/if the objective was met. Explain why or why not.

STUDENT TEXT

Technology Adaptation

- Age Calculation

  1. Multiply the first number of the age by 5. (If < 10—e.g., 5—consider it as 05. If it is > 100—e.g., 102—then take 10 as the first digit, 2 as the second one.)

  2. Add 3.

  3. Multiply by 2.

  4. Add the second digit of the age.

  5. Subtract 6.

  6. Ask students to read what is on their screens. (The answer should come out as the user's age.)

- Always 73

  1. Choose a four-digit number and enter it twice (e.g., 4356 would be entered 43564356). Make sure the students remember the original four-digit number.

- Divide by 137.

- Divide by the original four-digit number.

- The answer will always be 73, no matter what four-digit combination they choose (except for 0000 of course).

UNIT III
GETTING THE TIMING DOWN

Sequencing is a thinking skill that helps students to organize information in relation to time. This skill, which we call "getting the timing down," is important for students to learn as they become aware of patterns within narratives and how such patterns relate to cause and effect.

The exercises in this unit introduce students to the concept and the skill of sequencing. Students will also use sequencing skills to predict outcomes based on knowledge of prior events in a narrative.

Sequencing may include putting events in order (chronological), writing steps in order (e.g., instructions, recipes), and organizing a passage of text to improve understanding.

Students' experiences with these exercises will provide insight into how students organize and use their own sense of timing.

STUDENT TEXT

Introduction

When you read or hear a story, you can understand it better if you know the order in which the events are taking place. Knowing the order of events means that you know what happened first, what happened next, and so on.

Another way of saying this is that you know the *sequence* of events.

"Getting the timing down" means to understand the sequence of events in a story. Sequencing may include putting events in order (chronological), writing steps in order (e.g., instructions, recipes), and organizing a passage of text to improve understanding.

The exercises in this unit will help you learn more about "getting the timing down" or *sequencing*.

Suggested Directions for Unit III

Class Period I

1. Students can complete the exercises in this unit individually, in pairs, or in small groups. Students may want to do some of these exercises alone and others with a partner or partners.

2. Read the introduction for Unit III out loud, or have a student or students read it aloud. Discuss briefly for clarity and emphasis.

STUDENT TEXT

Exercise I: Philip's Story—What's the Sequence of Events?

Directions: Read the paragraphs that follow, and complete all italicized instructions.

Refer to the map of Philip's neighborhood. Philip lives in the last house on the right side of Torrey Avenue as you are heading west. *Mark his house so you can see where he lives.*

Philip has many errands to do, and he only has a short time before he has to pick up his sister, Anne, at the day care center.

You will see a list of Philip's errands. *First read over all of the errands.* You can use your map as a reference as you read them. *Then figure out in what sequence Philip should do his errands so he can do them as quickly as possible.* Marking the map in pencil may be helpful to you.

When you have decided on a sequence, number the errands so they will show the sequence of events. In the space on the left of each errand, mark the first errand #1, the second #2, and so on.

A. __5__ Philip is hungry. He buys a double scoop pistachio and chocolate ice cream cone at CHUCK'S.

B. __4__ Philip wants to see *The Hunger Games*, which is playing at the THEATER tonight. He stops to buy two tickets.

C. __8__ Philip takes his little sister, Anne, to DONNA'S KENNELS to look at the puppies.

D. __1__ Philip decides to ride his bike so he can do everything faster. The tires need air. Before he can do anything else, he goes to F.B. GARAGE to fill his tires.

E. __9__ Philip brings Anne home. He listens to music and relaxes. It's been a long afternoon, but it's all over now.

F. __3__ Philip wants to play baseball this year, so he stops to register at WELLINGTON FIELD. He notices the theater's billboard across the street.

G. __7__ Philip has to pick up his little sister, Anne, at C.T.'s DAYCARE. Anne begs to see the puppies at DONNA'S KENNELS.

H. __6__ Philip drops two overdue books off at the LIBRARY. He doesn't go in to pay for them because he still has ice cream on his hands.

I. __2__ DORIE'S COOKIE FACTORY sells day-old cookies at half price. Philip's mother wants him to pick up a pound of cookies, so he does.

3. Read aloud the directions to Exercise I, "Philip's Story," to the students. Then have the students work on the exercise. (With a young class, read the paragraphs and instructions aloud and discuss how to begin the exercise.)

When your students have completed the exercise, go over their answers. Discuss how students developed their sequence of events. A "correct" sequence is shown in italics. Students may develop other sequences. In the class discussion, be sure to talk about why one sequence can be more "correct" than others.

STUDENT TEXT

PHILIP'S NEIGHBORHOOD

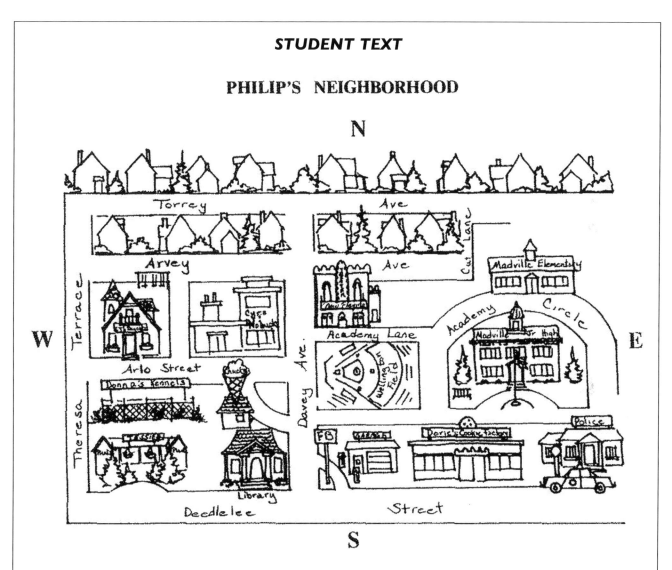

Key Words: Time Qualifiers

When you read or listen to a story, you will often find key words that can give you an idea about *when* events in the story take place. These key words are *time qualifiers*. These words qualify other words or phrases. To qualify is to make the meaning of words or phrases clearer.

(continued)

Some examples of *time qualifiers* that tell you more about when events take place are these:

while	during	before
after	as	until
following	afterward	in the meantime

There are many other *time qualifiers*. Any word or phrase that helps you to understand when events are happening is a *time qualifier*.

4. Have the students read "Key Words: Time Qualifiers," or read it aloud to them. Discuss briefly. Then go over the directions for Exercise II orally. Do the two examples as a class. Then have the students complete the exercise. Go over the sentences, and discuss.

STUDENT TEXT

Exercise II

Directions: Each of the sentences that follow includes two events. In each sentence, circle the word(s) that you recognize as a *time qualifier*. Then underline the event that happens first. If the events in a sentence are happening at the same time, do not underline anything.

Example

Before <u>Molly left for school</u>, she ate two pieces of toast. We set up the tents while the others gathered firewood. I had a great time **after** <u>I got to know all of the people there.</u>

1. **Before** Miguel had realized the danger he was in, <u>he was enjoying sailing over the wild waves.</u>

2. Amanda searched for clues to the disappearance of her brother, Cody, but in the meantime, he slept soundly, unaware that she was trying to find him.

3. <u>It had taken years of hard work</u>, but **finally** the statue was finished.

4. **Following** <u>the wedding ceremony</u>, there was a reception at the Martin Luther King Community Center.

5. Water expands **when** <u>it is cooled</u>.

6. As the ice masses drew back, they carved lakes and hills on the earth's surface.

7. <u>Divide the money equally among yourselves</u>, and **then** go to the store.

8. All during the time I had been outdoors planting, the baby had been playing happily in her pen.

9. <u>The water pressure built up</u> **until** the dam finally cracked.

(continued)

Finding Clues to the Timing

Sometimes the events described in a story are not in a sequence. The author may tell one part of the story and then jump into the past or the future. When an author jumps around in time like this, she or he must give clues to help the reader understand what is happening. Often these clues are *time qualifiers*.

When you are reading or listening to a story, pay attention to the *time qualifiers*. They can help you understand what happened and when it happened. This helps you to follow the story better.

Class Period 2

1. Read "Finding Clues to the Timing." Discuss briefly. You may want to review the *time qualifiers* from the previous lesson.

2. Have the students do Exercise III individually, or read it aloud to them. It may be beneficial to read Exercise III aloud so students can benefit from more practice in using the listening skills introduced in the first two units. When the students have completed the exercise, go over it with the class, first discussing the order of events in the story and then reviewing the time qualifiers in the passage.

STUDENT TEXT

Exercise III

Directions: While reading the story, pay close attention to the time qualifiers. Underline each time qualifier. Then number the events listed in the order in which they happened. Number the first event #1, the second event #2, and so on.

The skies were heavy with thick gray clouds. It was only three o'clock. <u>Still early</u>, Nick thought, so he'd have plenty of time to get home. <u>Earlier</u> this morning Nick had listened to the weather report. The weather people had predicted a major snowstorm. From the looks of the sky, he was sure that the prediction would come true.

Nick was excited. He loved the snow. The prospect of walking home in the snowstorm did not bother him at all. He was well bundled and had just a little less than a mile to go. The path through the woods was completely clear. If it did snow, it would be the first snow of the season.

<u>After</u> Nick had been walking for about ten minutes, thick flakes began to swirl around him. <u>Long ago</u>, when he was in preschool, his teacher had told the class that each flake that fell from the sky was different. <u>Ever since then</u>, Nick had tried to find two flakes that were exactly alike. He hadn't found them yet, but he was sure that of the millions that fell from the sky, if he kept looking, he would find the magical pair. He'd always told himself that when he found them, he would get whatever he'd wish for.

Nick was so busy catching and examining the lovely flakes that he didn't notice that the storm was intensifying. The swirling flakes had gathered force. The forest path was now a line of white winding through the tall pines. But Nick was not concentrating on the gathering forces of the snow. He was mesmerized by the thought of finding the two identical flakes. He stopped in his favorite spot, a clearing beneath two sycamore trees, so that he would have more light to examine the snow.

(continued)

By the time he gave some attention to what was happening around him, the snow had become thick. It was so thick, in fact, that he could barely make out the outline of the trees around the clearing. He became a bit alarmed as he remembered his mother telling him, "Nick, this will be our first winter here. The storms in these parts come up quickly. You don't get the same warning as we did back east. Soon the ground is covered, and you can't see your hand in front of your face."

At the time Nick thought his mother was being a bit overly cautious. Not even here in the Midwest could a storm sneak up that quickly on a boy who had experienced snowstorms all his life. But as Nick searched for the path that should now continue through a grove of maples, he knew his mother had been right to warn him.

Still, he wasn't worried. He was very close to home after all, and the snow was just beginning to cover the ground. He did, however, quicken his pace. In his haste and because the snow made the forest a new, strange world, Nick took the wrong turn. He had gone half a mile when he discovered that he was heading toward the pond, not the old farmhouse that his family had moved into last summer.

The storm was lashing out in all its fury. Nick couldn't see the nose in front of his face, much less his hand. The maple and ash trees no longer protected the winding path. Now Nick was worried. He raced in what he thought was the right direction. It was getting dark. Soon he would not even have the comfort of daylight.

"Whatever am I going to do?" thought Nick as he admitted to himself that he didn't know if he was heading home or in some wild circle toward the pond. He was growing tired, and he realized that he'd have to catch his breath and think clearly before going on. He pulled his coat away from his watch to see how much time he would have left before total darkness was upon him. Instead of looking at his watch, he saw, wide-eyed, two snowflakes that for all the world looked perfectly alike. Here was the chance to test his theory.

"Oh, I wish I could find my way home!"

Just then, his dog, Buddy, bounded into his arms. He was a great German shepherd with an amazing sense of direction. Nick knew now he had found his way home.

a. __2__ Nick's family moved from the East.

b. __4__ The weather people had predicted a snowstorm.

c. __3__ Nick's mother had warned him about midwestern snowstorms.

d. __1__ Nick's preschool teacher had told him no two snowflakes were alike.

e. __7__ The storm was intensifying.

f. __8__ Nick noticed the powerful storm.

g. __6__ Nick was looking for a pair of identical snowflakes.

h. __5__ It was three o'clock in the afternoon.

i. __10__ Nick's dog, Buddy, found him.

j. __9__ Nick had taken the wrong turn.

Predicting Outcomes

When you are reading or listening to a story, you can use *time qualifiers* to help you understand the sequence of events. Then when you know what has already happened, you can often figure out what will happen next in the story.

(continued)

Figuring out what will probably happen next is called *predicting outcomes*. When you predict an outcome, you use what you already know about a story to make a "good guess" about what will happen next.

Trying to *predict outcomes* also helps you to become actively involved in whatever you're hearing or reading.

When you predict an outcome, you ask yourself questions and try to answer them before you read or are told what happens.

3. Read "Predicting Outcomes" aloud to the students, or have a student or students read it aloud. Discuss for clarity and emphasis.

STUDENT TEXT

Exercise IV

Directions: Read the following paragraphs. Underline the *time qualifiers* that help you to think about the possible outcome of each story. Then answer the question that follows each paragraph.

1. <u>When</u> I awoke this morning, the sun was shining brightly in a clear, blue sky. I was excited because this was the day I had planned for the big picnic. <u>After</u> breakfast I turned on the radio and heard the weather report: "A moist cold front will be traveling rapidly across the Pacific Northwest. This front will push out the high currently settled over our region and will bring heavy rain. Rains <u>will continue</u> into tomorrow." When I looked at the mountain to the west, I saw billowing black clouds.

   Do you think this person will have a picnic on this day? What makes you think this?

   Answers may vary.

---

4. Read the directions for Exercise IV aloud to the students, and have them begin the exercise. Circulate among the students as they work on their predictions. Help them figure out ways to make predictions. Stress that there is no right or wrong answer.

5. Go over Exercise IV as a class. Discuss the students' predictions.

STUDENT TEXT

2. My teacher asked me to do an experiment to prove that a vacuum, or empty space, can't exist if there is something available to fill it. I knew that a candle needed oxygen to burn, and I also knew that oxygen took up space. So I put a candle in a shallow bowl and put an inch of water into the bowl. When I put a glass jar over the candle, I knew the candle would go out after it had used up all the oxygen within the jar. Then, with all the oxygen gone, the empty space within the jar would need to be filled, if possible, with another substance.

   Predict what will happen to the water in the bowl. Explain your prediction.

   Answers will vary.

(*continued*)

3. They say that if you don't learn from your mistakes, then "history will repeat itself." I never knew what that meant until I figured out there was a reason why I kept turning up on the "lost list." The first time I got lost, I had an excuse: I was only five years old. My mother had said, "Stay right here while Mama tries this dress on." I didn't listen to her. Instead I followed a cart full of toys. I should have learned to listen from that experience, but I didn't. I was seven when the teacher told our class to report to the auditorium after lunch. Again I wasn't listening, so I spent the better part of the afternoon looking for my class. When it finally came time for our class trip to Montreal, I was really excited. I was also determined not to get lost, but as I said, "History has a way of repeating itself."

Do you think the writer gets lost in Montreal? Why do you think the way you do?

Answers may vary.

4. In 1641 the population of New France was 240. Most of the people living there were single soldiers. French officials asked unmarried women to come to the New World to become soldiers' wives. Ships soon arrived in New France carrying more than 150 female immigrants. Then the government offered special rewards for large families. If people had ten children, they received a pension. Girls were given large sums if they married before they were sixteen. Boys who married before the age of twenty also received special rewards.

Predict the population of New France in 1675. What makes you think this?

Answers may vary.

Additional Suggestions

1. Develop ways in which students can use their sequencing skills as a part of the regular curriculum. The more experience students have in working with the sequences, the more competent they will become in employing these skills. Some of the ways to do this are the following:

   a. Write out flowcharts for certain class procedures, instructions for a school fire drill or storm drill.

   Suggest other activities that lend themselves to the use of flowcharts, such as revising written work, choosing a spelling team, figuring out why a science experiment didn't work and restructuring the experiment, and so on. In working with sequencing, focus your students' attention on the "stable points" in a sequence: beginnings and ends, events that are directly connected, and obvious "befores" and "afters."

   b. Read a novel to the class. Read for a certain amount of time each day. At the end of each reading, discuss the clues that will structure the events of the next reading. Invite students to predict what could happen.

   c. Suggest some formulas for writing factual responses. These can be helpful when the students want to prove a point or stage a discussion. Such formulas might look like this:

   I think that cell phones are harmful/helpful to me as a person who is learning a lot about the world now. In the first place, the most important thing about using a cell phone is

Then, you must consider that cell phones _____

_____

In addition to the examples listed, cell phones can be _____

_____

In summary, I would like to stress that cell phones_____

_____

Be careful not to overuse these formulas as they apply best to certain subject matter and learning styles. Many students can be inhibited by too much formulated writing. It is also well worth the time and effort spent to help students generate the formulas themselves.

2. Time qualifiers can provide students with one kind of clue in recognizing and understanding sequences. *Connectors* offer another kind of clue. *Connectors* are words that connect ideas together. They can indicate some action or event has already taken place. They can also inform about sequences not in time but in the organization of a passage. For example, in the following sentence, *another one* is a connector: Another one of the Fox's clever tricks was flattery.

Introduce the idea of *connectors* to students. Then have them read a passage in which the paragraphs are out of the correct order, like the one below. Ask students to circle the *connectors* in these paragraphs and then place the paragraphs in the correct order by numbering them.

_3_ **Another** woman who tricked the British was Dicey Langston of South Carolina. She was only fifteen when she became a self-appointed spy. She would watch British military maneuvers from her farm and report to the Patriots. The British were slow to realize that a young girl was the source of so many information leaks.

_2_ **One** of the underestimated women was Nancy Hart. British soldiers burst into her home demanding to be fed. She sent her daughter next door to get some water and warn the Patriots. By the time the Patriots arrived with her daughter, Nancy Hart had stolen the British rifles, killed one soldier, and cornered the rest of them.

_1_ **At the time** of the Revolutionary War, most people expected women to remain quiet, obedient, and in the background of manly pursuits. This idea got many British soldiers in trouble because these soldiers underestimated the strength and cunning of American women.

_4_ Probably the most famous of all women Patriots was Deborah Sampson. **Unlike the other two women mentioned,** she didn't set out to fool the British by appearing to be a weak female. She dressed herself as a man and fought for three years in the army. Her identity was discovered only when she needed to be nursed for a high fever. She was then dismissed, for even the Patriots underestimated the power of a fighting woman.

3. Take newspaper articles or stories from workbooks. Cut them up, and code them in a way that will allow them to be put together. Then mount them on cardboard so that they can withstand some handling. Give four stories to a group of three to four students. Mix up the cards. Challenge the group to put the story parts in the correct pile as well as the correct sequence.

4. Give the students the end of a story such as the following:

A man was found dead in what appeared to be a poorly dug, shallow ditch.

Challenge the students to discover the rest of the story by asking questions. Explain that they may only ask questions that can be answered by "yes" or "no." Also note that they must listen carefully to each other's questions and your answers.

Students will ask questions that explore various story threads, or sequences, until they can reconstruct the entire story.

The remainder of the story begun above is the following:

A man was hiking in early spring. He had not paid any attention to the avalanche warnings that the park had posted. He wandered off into a danger zone where a huge boulder rolled down the mountain at a tremendous speed, carving a path as it went. The boulder hit him, and he was killed instantaneously.

STUDENT TEXT

Unit III Summary

"Getting the timing down" means understanding the order of events in a story. The order in which things take place in a story is also called the *sequence* of events.

When you read or listen to a story, you can recognize key words that tell you about when events take place. These words are called *time qualifiers*. Some examples of time qualifiers are these: *after, before, until, while, following, during*.

You can use your ability to "get the timing down" to understand when things happen in a story and to *predict outcomes*. This means to use what you already know about the sequence of events in a story to figure out what will probably happen next. By trying to predict outcomes when reading or listening, readers are more active and involved.

Ask students to read the summary silently. After they have finished reading, facilitate a class discussion based on what was learned in this unit.

Suggested Retrieval Activities

As part of closure and retrieval of information learned, ask students to do one or more of the following:

- Pose some questions that can be answered thumbs up/down/sideways. Ask for an explanation of the decision.

- Ask students to explain the relevancy of the concept of "timing" to their lives or how they might use it.

- Ask students to write a jingle about what was learned from this unit.

STUDENT TEXT

Technology Adaptation

- Develop a timeline of major events in your life.

  1. When were you born?

  2. What school did you attend first and when?

  3. Have you ever won anything, placed in an event, or received a trophy or ribbon?

These are just examples. The timeline will be about you.

Use a program like SmartArt in Microsoft Office or search "timeline maker" on the Internet to use a free program.

- Search for a recipe online. Copy and paste a recipe you found for "homemade yeast rolls" into a word-processing program. Rearrange the order of directions and explain why changing the order might make a difference in the outcome of the finished bread.

Books Involving Timing Sequence

Goldilocks and the Three Bears

The Three Little Pigs

Seven Blind Mice

The Wizard of Oz

UNIT IV
A MATTER OF TIME

The activities in this unit help students begin to understand how they make sense of time and how they can begin to control their own use of time through planning—specifically, how a student can use a calendar or agenda as a tool to assist in this process. This unit will provide students a greater awareness of how they perceive time and begin to practice a method for keeping track of their time.

Some students will probably enjoy making and using a schedule. Others may not. We suggest introducing students to the idea of a schedule as a tool for one's own use, not as an obligation that one does for others. We have found that setting this unit within such a framework can help to lessen any resistance that students feel about learning how to make and use a schedule. We will also explore how using tools such as an agenda can greatly increase productivity of students, and help them become more organized.

STUDENT TEXT

Introduction

Think about the meaning of the word *time*. Can you give a definition for this word? Does this word have more than one meaning for you?

Write your definition for the word *time* on the lines below. If you can think of more than one definition, write two or three.

time: _____

_____

_____

_____

_____

_____

(continued)

You may have found it difficult to define the word *time*. Time is not something we can touch, see, or smell. Yet we can "feel" time or sense it as it passes. And we can also "hear" time or sense the order in a piece of music.

Our sense of time seems to change as we grow older. For instance, when we are younger, time seems to pass by slowly like when playing with friends or doing something fun. As we get older, time in school, for example, seems to pass slowly and free time seems to pass by more quickly. Think about the last time you took a nap—the time probably went by faster than you wanted it to! Then imagine the amount of time you needed, but maybe did not spend, when studying for your last test at school. With proper planning, you can use time and time management with tools like a calendar or agenda to provide you ample time for all activities. This unit will help you to look more carefully at what time is, how you use your time, and how to plan.

Suggested Directions for Unit IV

Class Period 1

1. Read through this unit carefully before teaching it. Younger students may need more assistance when making a time log for the first time. Consider providing examples with the entire class as an example.

2. Encourage students to use a pencil when completing their time log. This allows them to erase and make changes without starting over.

3. Have students read the introduction and write their definition(s). Discuss the various definitions of *time*.

4. Divide the class into small groups of 3–4 students. Tell them they will do Exercise I individually but will discuss it in their groups. Provide ample time for students to complete the list, assign time values, and total the results.

5. Once all students in a group are finished, each student should star the top five events requiring the most time in the day.

6. Have the small student groups come up with a single list of the top events for their entire group to share.

7. To generate whole-class participation, make a tally of major activities (e.g., top five), calling on each group and writing the results on the board. You may also have one "reporter" from each group list their group results and then tally the group lists as a class.

STUDENT TEXT

Exercise I

Directions: Read the directions and then complete the time log using a pencil. Total the number of hours and minutes spent in a typical day. Your total should be approximately 24 hours (1 day).

(continued)

How do you spend your time? You may not remember everything you do in the course of the day, but there are 24 hours for everyone! Some events are routine and occur daily or weekly, while some events are special and only occur occasionally. Some events happen in just a few minutes while others can take several hours. On the following log, reflect and make a good guess about how much time you spend each day on each activity. It is a list of suggested activities only. You may want to personalize this list to your own needs. Assign a time (hours or minutes) to the list using the blank space provided for each activity listed. On the blank lines (at the bottom of the suggested list), add your own personal activities specific to you. Cross out anything that does not apply to you. There are no right or wrong answers.

Time Spent	Activity
_____	Get ready in the morning
_____	Eat breakfast
_____	Feed/water pets
_____	Attend school
_____	Eat lunch
_____	Participate in sports/clubs
_____	Do homework
_____	Eat dinner
_____	Text friends
_____	Read
_____	Spend time with friends
_____	Listen to music
_____	Clean your room
_____	Watch TV
_____	Play a video game
_____	Sleep
_____	_____
_____	_____
_____	_____
_____	TOTAL TIME (should be approximately 24 hours)

(continued)

Now, be more specific and specify the amount of time you spend on each subject during the school day. List the name for the subject/class and the amount of time you spend there.

Time Spent   Subject Name/Class

_____   _____

_____   _____

_____   _____

_____   _____

_____   _____

_____   _____

_____   _____

_____   _____

_____   TOTAL TIME

A String of Events—Planning the Steps

When you have a certain project in mind such as making a craft, assembling something, or getting a book report ready for school, you often think through the things you need to do—or steps you need to take to complete the project. What's the first step? The second one? And so on.

For instance, if you want to do your book report, you think about all the things that need to be done before you can write a final draft. Some of those things might be:

- read the book

- discuss the book with your teacher

- outline the main events

- outline the main characters

- write a rough draft

You must have a clear idea of the project you wish to do. You must also think of the steps you need to take in order to get this project done. It is helpful to think of these steps as a string of events. In other words, all the steps you take

(continued)

and the order in which you take them must have a logical connection. You cannot outline the main events of the book until you have read the book.

Exercise II

Directions: Look at the example and events 1–2. The steps that are listed below each number are not in the correct order.

Suggest a better order by numbering the first thing to be done as #1, and the second thing as #2, and so on.

Example: Make pancakes

    a.   _5_   mix ingredients

    b.   _4_   heat skillet

    c.   _2_   read recipe

    d.   _8_   eat pancakes

    e.   _1_   find recipe

    f.   _3_   get out necessary ingredients

    g.   _6_   put mixture in hot, greased skillet

    h.   _7_   flip pancakes

Event # 1—Pick out a birthday present

    a.   _4_   wrap the present

    b.   _2_   check to see if I have enough money to buy the present

    c.   _6_   give the present to my friend

    d.   _3_   go shopping

    e.   _1_   find out what my friend wants/needs

    f.   _5_   attend the birthday party

Event # 2—Plan to see a movie

    a.   _4_   text or call my friend

    b.   _1_   check available movies online or use a movie/show app

(continued)

c. _6_   suggest going to a movie together

d. _2_   check to see if I have enough money

e. _3_   get permission from parents

f. _5_   arrange a ride to the movie

Event # 3—Setting goals using time helps motivate you to get something done, especially those tasks you may not want to do. As you work on schoolwork, for example, set goals where you can reward yourself when something is accomplished. For this example, we will use your daily homework. Let's assume you have an average of one hour of homework each weeknight. Using the list from Exercise I, list the top five activities you enjoy doing the most:

Time Spent   Activity

_____   _____

_____   _____

_____   _____

_____   _____

_____   _____

Now, we are going to balance what you like to do with your homework time. For the purposes of this exercise, we are going to start your free time after school ends for the day until your usual bedtime. In the space provided, list how many hours (average) you have each day from the time school ends to the time you go to bed.

_____

_____

_____

This time you have remaining time to decide how you want to spend it. Assuming you have one hour of time for homework each night, how can you adjust your desired activities to account for this? On the list below, reorganize your time allowed for each activity allowing for one hour of homework time.

Time Spent   Activity

_____   _____

_____   _____

_____   _____

_____   _____

_____   _____

Class Period 2

1. Have a student or students read "A String of Events—Planning the Steps," or read it aloud to the class. Discuss briefly.

2. Read over the directions to Exercise II with the class. Do the example together. This exercise may be done as a class activity or in small groups. Have students share their answers. Discuss as necessary.

STUDENT TEXT

Exercise III

Directions: Using a weekly calendar, record your class each day by subject for one week. It is strongly encouraged for you to record *all* events that take 10 minutes or longer in your day including chores, activities, and so on. Practice completing your agenda or log by starting on the current day.

Weekly Calendar

Monday, [Day]	
Tuesday, [Day]	
Wednesday, [Day]	
Thursday, [Day]	
Friday, [Day]	
Saturday, [Day]	
Sunday, [Day]	

Class Periods 3–10

1. Have students record their class assignments each day by subject in an agenda or daily log. If the school provides a printed student planner, encourage students to use that tool. If this is not provided, an example of a reproducible weekly calendar is provided.

2. Encourage students to record all events that take 10 minutes or longer including chores, activities, and so on, discussed in previous exercises.

3. Using a document camera, show students how to complete the log by providing an all-class example.

4. Let students practice with the current day to get started.

5. From the time this exercise is assigned until one week has passed, check with students daily to see if they have or have not completed this.

6. Reproduce blank weekly calendars provided in this booklet for students (if needed).

STUDENT TEXT

Using Your Agenda/Time Log: What Happened?

How did you spend your time this past week? After reviewing your results, you may be surprised how you spent your time. Think about the questions below and then answer them honestly.

1. Did anything get in the way of my schedule? (If things did get in the way, what were they?)

   _____

   _____

   _____

   _____

2. Did I get everything done that I wanted to do?

   _____

   _____

   _____

   _____

3. What did I spend the most time doing this past week?

   _____

   _____

   _____

   _____

(continued)

---

4. How could I make better use of my time?

_____

_____

_____

_____

5. How does using this agenda/time log seem helpful to me?

_____

_____

_____

_____

6. What was not helpful from these exercises and why?

_____

_____

_____

_____

Class Period 11

1. After students have finished recording class assignments and/or other activities, have them complete "Using Your Planner/Time Log: What Happened?" Have students discuss their results in small groups and then with the class.

Additional Suggestions

1. Provide students with at least one structured experience in making and using a schedule beyond the exercises in this unit. Assign a project for the class. Ask students to draw up a schedule for completion of the project. Then let them go ahead and work on the project. When students hand in their completed projects, also ask them to evaluate their own schedules and how useful they were in completing the work of the project.

2. Post a large calendar with school and class deadlines. You may also want to get smaller copies of the same calendar for three-ring binders. Encourage students to write in their own deadlines and important activities.

3. Have students interview the adults in various professions to see how they schedule their time. Have them report to the class the various systems of scheduling that they discover. Encourage them to try ways of scheduling that are interesting to them.

4. Make a collection of commercial calendars/planners of various sorts and sizes. Invite students to peruse them, and discuss with students how and why different formats serve different uses for these planners.

5. If your school does not have a common school planner, engage students in designing a calendar/planner for sale at school.

STUDENT TEXT

Unit IV Summary

- Keeping an agenda or time log will help you get organized with your time.

- Specifically, this unit provided tools to help you identify how you spend your time, how to plan, and how to set time goals for things you have to do and for things you want to do.

- Time is a delicate act of balancing since there are only 24 hours in each day. Recording daily events (including school subjects/assignments) in an agenda or time log provides a detailed record of how you spend your day. This exercise allows you to determine what adjustments might be needed to ensure you are maximizing time on task. This will allow you more time to do the fun things you enjoy.

- Keeping this daily log also creates a good habit you will hopefully continue in the future.

Suggested Retrieval Activities

As part of closure and retrieval of information learned, ask students to do one or more of the following:

- Consider requiring students to log more than one week as outlined in the lesson. Once a few days or weeks have been logged, encourage students to refer to previous entries and see if how they spend time has changed over a period of time.

- Have students share their daily log with friends in the class to determine similarities and differences in their agenda/daily log and how each person spends time on activities.

STUDENT TEXT

Technology Adaptation

- Use an online calendar program to keep track of your daily log.

- If you have a smart phone or other device available, investigate free apps about time management and scheduling. Keep a daily log of entries on how you spend your time each day.

- Use an electronic calendar program using your device to keep track of your day.

UNIT V
PUTTING IDEAS TOGETHER

Putting ideas together by categorization is an important foundation skill. First we need to help students learn to see the interrelatedness of detail before we can expect them to develop the skills involved in relating concepts.

Observe students as they read an assigned text. It may be surprising to discover that many read without trying to organize the information in their reading in any way. To help students learn to understand the relationship between categories and their parts, we need to teach them the necessary skills.

This unit provides an initial experience in learning the skill of categorization. It also helps students to learn how they can remember information more effectively when it is organized into categories.

STUDENT TEXT

Exercise I

Directions: Look at the words in group A. Then answer the questions below the list. List the letters of phrases or sentences that you choose. You do not need to copy the phrase or sentence itself. Do the same for group B.

Group A

    a. go to the store

    b. return a book to the library

    c. take out the trash

    d. pick up laundry

    e. text Sarah

    f. play a video game

(*continued*)

---

1. Which phrase(s) fit into the category of chores?

   Take out the trash and pick up laundry

2. Which phrase(s) fit into the category of errands?

   Go to the store and return a book to the library

3. Which phrase(s) fit into the category of things to do in my free time?

   Text Sarah and play a video game

4. Name a category in which all of these phrases fit.

   Answers may vary.

Group B

a. examining animal characteristics and behavior

b. analyzing data gathered from telescope observation

c. finding cures for diseases

d. writing observations

e. collecting information

f. studying climate

1. Which phrase(s) fit into the category of a scientist's job?

   Collecting information

2. Which phrase(s) fit into the category of ways that meteorologists (scientists who study the weather) make predictions?

   Analyzing data gathered from telescope observation and studying climate

3. Which phrase(s) fit into the category of an animal behaviorist's job?

   Writing observations and examining animal characteristics and behavior

4. Name a category in which all of these phrases fit.

   Collecting information

Suggested Directions for Unit V

1. Have students complete Exercise I. Have students do part or all of the exercise individually or in pairs. Then go over the exercise in class. Discuss any categories that gave students in the class any problems.

STUDENT TEXT

Exercise II

Directions: Organize the following words into as many categories as possible. List the categories and the words grouped within them in the spaces provided. You must list at least three words in each category that you create. You may use the same word in more than one category.

Try to create categories that no one else will!

star	see	lobster	crow	man	walnut
treasure	creator	wave	stove	woman	October
July	fox	mountain	pocket	crazy	September
drummer	potato	cashew	strawberry	highway	volcano
earthquake	ax	hammer	dog	queen	meteor
goat	stew	sloppy	sponge	August	rat
Octopus	river	ostrich	crater	square	June
saw	stone	fish	earth	ribbon	drill
valley	shark	November	onion	canary	hill
rake	whale				

---

2. Divide the class into small groups of 3–4 students. Read the directions for Exercise II aloud, or have a student read them. Stress that there must be three words in each category. This exercise can be modified from an individual to a group assignment by giving each group a point for each category it has created that is not mentioned by any other group.

    Have each group list its categories on the board. Discover which individuals or groups have created unique categories. Accept any reasonable answers.

CATEGORY_____ Words_____ _____ _____ _____	CATEGORY_____ Words_____ _____ _____ _____
CATEGORY_____ Words_____ _____ _____ _____	CATEGORY_____ Words_____ _____ _____ _____
CATEGORY_____ Words_____ _____ _____ _____	CATEGORY_____ Words_____ _____ _____ _____
CATEGORY_____ Words_____ _____ _____ _____	CATEGORY_____ Words_____ _____ _____ _____
CATEGORY_____ Words_____ _____ _____ _____	CATEGORY_____ Words_____ _____ _____ _____
CATEGORY_____ Words_____ _____ _____ _____	CATEGORY_____ Words_____ _____ _____ _____

Additional Suggestions

1. Use categorization as a way to preview a new lesson or unit. For example, write "Living Things" on the board and say, "We are going to study a unit about living things today. Can you name some living things?" Students will undoubtedly generate a long list of living things. Then discuss categories within the topic of living things, and have the class organize the items on the list into appropriate categories.

2. Collect many small items. For example: a paper clip, toothpicks, egg cartons, coins, forks, spools of thread, and so on. Put students in small groups of 3–5 students. Have students categorize the items in as many ways as possible. Ask them to name the categories into which these things fit. Have them "play around" with some of the concepts of categorization. For instance, if there is a category of utensils found at home, then cooking utensils and sewing utensils equals the category of utensils found at home. In other words, encourage students to look at sets and subsets and the relationship between them.

3. Play games with students that emphasize categorization whenever there are a few available minutes in class. Some examples are these:

a. Play "Animal, Mineral, Vegetable" (also known as "Twenty Questions") with students. Think of an animal, mineral, or vegetable. Allow students to ask twenty "yes" and "no" questions to try to guess the animal, mineral, or vegetable. They will need to use categorization to ask effective questions.

b. Select a student volunteer and have them go to another room nearby (library, adjoining classroom, etc.) where there is a teacher and wait for a few minutes. Have the other students physically place themselves in categories such as: blond hair, over four feet tall, wearing shorts, with freckles, and so on. (You may want to guide the category choices and omit ones that may be sensitive.) Have the student return to the classroom and guess why the other students are arranged as they are.

c. Give students a list of words with one word that doesn't belong, such as the following:

Winter Activities	Dangerous Animals	Fruits
swim	bear	strawberries
ski	crocodile	corn
skate	kitten	oranges
sled	tiger	tomato
sculpt snow	lion	grapes

Have students name the category and find the word that doesn't belong. The students can make up similar lists and give them to each other.

4. Integrate the concept of categorization into whatever you are teaching. For example, if teaching a unit about plants, have students collect a number of plants and examine the characteristics of plants. Then the students could arrange the plants by categories.

5. Take out a number of books from the library from diverse categories: fiction, art, biography, sciences, travel, and so on. Cover the cataloging number on each book, and have your students organize the books by category.

STUDENT TEXT

Unit V Summary

A category is a name for a group of ideas or pieces of information that have something in common. For example, city, state, town, and village all fit into the category of units of government. When you organize ideas and information into categories, you can usually remember them better. Also you will discover how ideas and information are similar and how they are different.

Suggested Retrieval Activities

As part of closure and retrieval of information learned, ask students to do one or more of the following:

- Ask students to list the key ideas from the lesson and explain why each is important.

- Place students in small groups and ask each group to make a list of what was learned. Call on each group and ask them to explain one of their choices.

STUDENT TEXT

Technology Adaptation

- Choose artifact items from diverse categories such as: shells, coins, minerals, and so on. Organize the items by category. Search for pictures or articles of these items online and create a presentation to virtually display these items (and their categories) to the class.

- Take an inventory of items in the classroom. Develop categories and, using a computer, create a form using an application like Google Docs. In the form, record categories and lists. Then partner with another student and share the form. Identify similarities and differences in the categories based on your lists. Share the results in a presentation to the class.

- Use a class blog to explain why what you learned in the lesson is important.

UNIT VI
PICTURING IN YOUR MIND'S EYE

In our culture we tend not to value the ability to visualize or think by imaging. One reason for this undervaluing is that when children begin to develop verbal and other symbolic skills, we encourage them to use these skills in place of their imaginative abilities rather than in conjunction with them.

Another reason is that the very nature of thinking in images or visualizing makes the process difficult to put into words and therefore problematic to define and incorporate within our educational structures. A third reason is that our world of media and print does not require the individual to rely on her or his ability to image or "see with the mind's eye."

The exercises in this unit will help students with the process of visualization.

STUDENT TEXT

Exercise I

Directions: Your teacher will read a selection aloud called "The Body's Defense Against Disease." As you listen, try to picture the following things:

1. The first line of defense is described as an obstacle course. Try to picture the obstacles that get in the way of germs.

2. Part of the second line of defense is the white blood cells. Try to picture what the white blood cells look like as they surround a germ.

3. The third line of defense is antibodies. When you hear about antibodies, try to form a picture of them.

4. As you hear about the following things, try to get a picture of each one in your mind's eye: germs, lymph, capillaries, and infection.

When the reading is completed, you will be asked to answer some factual questions.

Again, it might help you to close your eyes so you can picture things without interference as you listen.

---

1. Have students write the answers to the questions including the section "For Fun." Ask students how imagining helped them answer the questions.

The Body's Defense Against Disease

Since germs are present everywhere, you might think it amazing that we are not ill all the time. The reason we are not is that the human body is armed to defend itself against infection and disease. The body has three lines of defense.

The first line of defense in the body is an obstacle course for germs. There are certain parts of your body that actually block germs from entering your bloodstream. These body parts are the skin, mucous in your nose and mouth, and stomach acids. The skin makes a thin but tough barrier for germs. When germs try to enter through the nose and mouth, thick mucous often blocks them. (That is the reason for your runny nose when you have a cold.) A final obstacle for the germs is stomach acids. It's difficult for the germs to get past these acids, which dissolve them in seconds.

If a germ should enter your bloodstream, however, you have an even more impressive force ready to do battle with the foreign invader. This is your second line of defense. An army of tiny white blood cells is always on the lookout for disease. The white blood cells themselves are so small that they squeeze through the walls of capillaries—the tiniest of blood vessels—to find the disease-causing germ. The white blood cells swarm around any foreign object such as a germ and devour it before it can do any harm to your body. Then a clear liquid in your blood called lymph washes away the digested germs and leftover white blood cells. During this struggle to free itself from germs, your body often gets overheated. The fever you develop wipes out the germs that need to live in low temperatures. Your body is now freed from the chance of infection.

Sometimes a germ does manage to get through the first two lines of defense. When this happens, your body's secret service springs into action. Your secret service is made up of antibodies that hide out in the blood cells until they need to be called into the fight. Each secret service agent or antibody is trained to fight off a certain germ. If that special germ gets through the first two lines of defense, the antibody charges out of hiding and surrounds and disintegrates the germ.

Of course, germs do sneak by and manage to make us sick at times. But our body's three lines of defense keep us pretty healthy when you consider the ever-present germ!

STUDENT TEXT

Answer These Questions

1. Name three things that provide an obstacle course in the body's first line of defense.

   Skin, mucous in your nose and mouth, stomach acids

2. How do white blood cells help the body protect you from germs?

   White blood cells surround the germ and disintegrate it

   (continued)

---

3. What is a capillary?

    The smallest of the blood vessels

4. What does an antibody do to protect you from germs?

    Antibodies are in the blood cells and are designed to fight off certain germs.

5. How does lymph help your body to handle germs?

    Lymph is a clear liquid that washes away the waste after germs have been disintegrated.

For Fun

1. Draw a germ as you pictured it.

2. Did any other interesting visual images come into your mind as you listened? If so, draw or explain them in words.

Kinds of Pictures in Your Mind's Eye

When people imagine, they often see pictures or images in their mind's eye. Sometimes the imagination includes other senses as well: hearing, smelling, touching, even tasting. In fact, when some people imagine, they don't see pictures at all. Instead they hear, smell, touch, taste, or all of these.

Everyone can imagine, but we all use our imagination in our own personal way. What do you experience when *you* imagine? Write your answer on the lines provided.

Answers may vary

2. Read aloud "Kinds of Pictures in Your Mind's Eye." Discuss briefly.

STUDENT TEXT

Solve Your Problems by Picturing the Steps

Sometimes you have an idea for a project you want to do. You can picture, or see in your mind's eye, a completed task. For example, you can imagine the tent when it is set up. You can imagine how to successfully play a video game. You can imagine how you might build a fort with plastic blocks.

However, when you start to work on the project, you find that the picture in your mind isn't as helpful as you had hoped. You don't know how to begin.

Exercise II

Directions: Following you will find three methods for making a paper airplane. Try to use each method, and discover which one works best for you. Use imagery to picture each step as you go.

Method I

Study the picture below. Then take one of the sheets that your teacher gave you. Try to construct the paper airplane pictured.

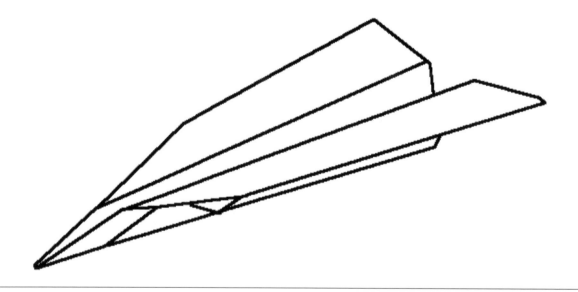

---

3. Read "Solve Your Problems by Picturing the Steps" aloud with your students.

Hand out three blank 8½" by 11" sheets of paper to each student. Read the directions for Exercise II aloud. Organize the students into pairs or small groups for this exercise. Explain that while the members of each pair or group should work together, each student should make her or his own airplane. When the students understand the instructions, have them begin the activity. As they work, circulate among them and give encouragement and help as needed. When the students have completed method III, give them a minute to fly their airplanes. Then engage them in discussing the three methods and how they used imagery.

STUDENT TEXT

Method II

Read the step-by-step instructions that follow. Complete each of the steps. Try to construct the paper airplane they describe.

Step 1

Use a sheet of 8½ × 11" paper. Crease-fold the paper in half first. Then open it. Fold the top corners down.

Step 2

Hold the paper lengthwise. Call the top left point A and the bottom left point B. Fold A and B down about a quarter of the sides to the crease. Make sure A and B touch on the center crease.

Step 3

Call the top points of the airplane's nose C and D. Fold in points C and D. The top two edges should meet each other on the center crease.

Step 4

Fold the entire airplane in half in the opposite direction.

Step 5

Fold the wings down to meet the bottom edge of the fuselage.

Step 6

Curl the tail section up slightly for better lift.

(continued)

Method III

Look at the pictures in the steps that follow. The pictures show what the airplane should look like *as* you follow the directions for each step. Try to match what you are doing to what you see.

Step 1

Use a sheet of 8½ × 11" paper. Crease-fold the paper in half first. Then open it. Fold the top corners down.

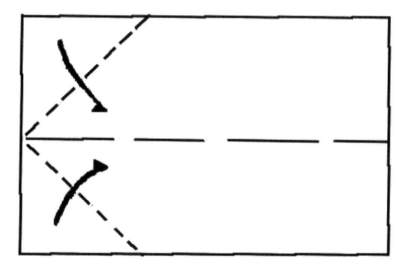

Step 2

Fold in the sides. Make sure that points A and B touch each other on the center crease.

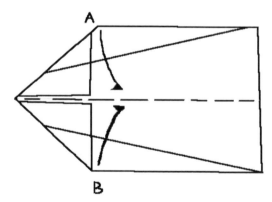

Step 3

Fold in points C and D. The top two edges should meet each other on the center crease.

(continued)

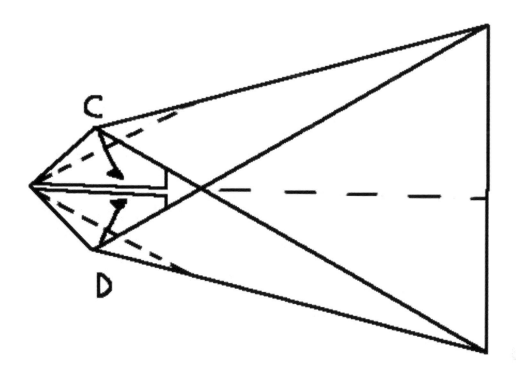

Step 4

Fold the entire airplane in half in the opposite direction.

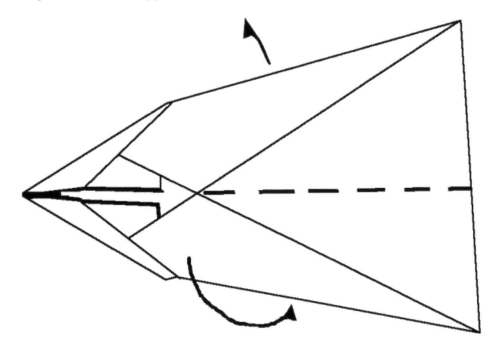

(*continued*)

Step 5

Fold the wings down to meet the bottom edge of the fuselage.

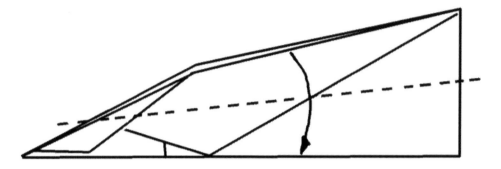

Step 6

Curl the tail section up slightly for better lift.

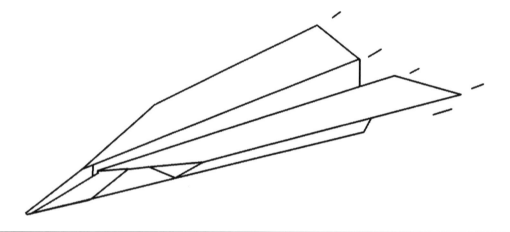

4. A good way to learn new vocabulary words is to use a three-column graphic organizer.

STUDENT TEXT

Directions: Fill in the graphic organizer with the following vocabulary words.

Word	Definition	Picture of Word
Antonym		
Base Word		
Capitalization		
Comma		
Conjunction		
Context Clues		
Editing		
Exposition		
Fact		
Fiction		
Interjection		

5. Read aloud the summary with students. Discuss for clarity and emphasis.

Additional Suggestions

1. Give the students diagrams of models (birdhouses, dollhouses, planes, cars, and so on). Ask them to study the diagrams and try to picture in their mind's eye what the completed model would look like. Then have the students describe what they imagine.

2. Give students a problem that forces them to visualize the building they are in. For example, tell them to imagine that they have been left alone in the building. All the windows and doors are locked with the exception of one. Be specific about the one window or door that is unlocked, and make this exit as far away and indirect as possible. Ask the students to imagine the fastest way to get out of the building using this exit.

3. Put students in pairs. Tell them they will be giving each other oral directions on how to get somewhere, but they will not know where their partner is taking them until the end of the directions. They must not draw diagrams or take notes. (Make sure the places chosen will be well known by all students.) Give each student a piece of paper with a destination written on it. Have students give each other directions without telling the partner the destination. The direction-giver is successful if his or her partner ends up knowing what his or her destination is.

   This game requires both the direction-giver and the direction-follower to use visual clues to construct a mental map.

4. Ask students to imagine the room they are sitting in from a different angle. For example, have the student in the first row imagine that she or he is in the last seat in the back row. See if he or she can picture the room from this new angle. Then have him or her go to the new place and see how accurate his or her imagination was.

   This kind of exercise is a good introduction to a creative writing assignment that requires a first-person character to describe different settings.

5. Have students make mental maps of their neighborhood or town. Ask them to close their eyes and imagine a walk from one point to another. Tell them to pay particular attention to anything they can sense (smell, touch, see, hear, taste) along the way. Give them at least five minutes to do this task. Then have students draw a diagram of what they imagined. Have students compare their diagrams.

6. Give students verbal tasks that are difficult to do, such as describing a spiral staircase, telling someone how to tie a shoe, explaining to someone how to focus a microscope, and so on. Invite them to develop creative ways to do these tasks.

7. Ask students to imagine doing a physical task before they actually enact it. For example, ask students to imagine they are about to pitch a ball. Ask them to imagine their body as it goes through each

stage of the process of pitching. Then have them a ball. Question them to see if they could use their imaging in the process of pitching.

8. View a documentary on a certain country or place to which most students have never traveled. Then discuss that setting in terms of categories beyond what the television can show. Talk about the aromas, the feel, the flavors, and the different scenes of the new place. Ask your students to imagine that they are visiting this place and to write a diary entry about a day in this place.

9. Read a novel that has been dramatized. Before watching the video dramatization, have your students discuss their image of the characters and settings. Then have students watch the dramatization. Critique the portrayal of character and setting by having the students compare the video images with the images they had previously formed.

10. Describe a scientific process, such as the division of cells. Encourage students to imagine this process. Then show a video depicting the process. Have the students compare their inner image to the video. Do this repeatedly with different processes to encourage the students' ability to visualize.

11. Get students to critique certain advertisements by discussing the power of visual imagery. Discuss the product as it is presented on the scene, and compare it to the actual product. Discuss how visual media encourages people to buy things they may not want or need.

12. The problems presented in this unit are concrete, spatial problems. However, visualization can also help on abstract levels. An example of this is when Archimedes climbed into the bathtub and shouted, "Eureka!" because he was finally able to imagine how the problem of weighing the king's gold could be solved. His own body's displacement of the water gave him the image he needed to solve the problem. Children also experience this "aha" phenomenon.

Explaining abstract scientific problems in a visual way often encourages children to use their intuition and ability to imagine. There are many scientific problems that lend themselves to a visual description.

- How does a prism break up white light into colors?

- How can certain weather conditions cause people to see mirages?

- How are a bee's eyes structured to highlight the flowers with the greatest honey-producing capacity?

Science can provide a wonderful context for inviting children to think both visually and intuitively.

13. After students have read a novel, ask them to become "movie producers." Ask them to think about where and how they would stage the story and what kinds of props, backdrops, and weather conditions they would need. Also, ask them to imagine what actresses or actors would be the most appropriate for the main characters.

STUDENT TEXT

Unit VI Summary

Most people have the ability to imagine or see pictures in their mind's eye. Sometimes the imagination uses your other senses: hearing, smelling, feeling, and even tasting.

These pictures or images can help to make reading and hearing stories more interesting to you. You can also remember important details when you form images of them.

The ability to picture things in your mind's eye is often helpful in solving problems. When you use your imagination to help you solve a problem, break the problem down into small, easy-to-do steps. Then do one step at a time.

Suggested Retrieval Activities

As part of closure and retrieval of information learned, ask students to do one or more of the following:

- Have students read a small section from a book or article (consider something the class is currently studying) and then give students a few minutes to daydream. Then, have students draw an image or describe an image if they are not comfortable drawing reflecting on the pictures they mentally visualized.

- Have students determine from their drawing or description which sense (taste, touch, smell, etc.) they felt was the most real to them in their mental image and discuss.

STUDENT TEXT

Technology Adaptation

- Draw pictures of vocabulary words using the computer program Paint (for Windows) or Paintbrush (for Mac).

UNIT VII
IMPROVING YOUR MEMORY

Throughout their school years, students are required to learn many different kinds of material. Yet they are rarely involved in instruction that can help them understand how learning takes place and how their own memories function.

The purpose of this unit is to help students learn about the workings of human memory and begin to develop several memory skills. Students are introduced to the concepts of short-term and long-term memory and presented with several methods for "moving" information from short-term into long-term memory.

Students are also introduced to several mnemonic methods. Mnemonics is based on scientifically validated principles of how the human memory works. Although mnemonics has been part of our culture for many years, schools have tended to ignore its potential value to students.

If you are not familiar with mnemonics, be sure to examine this unit carefully before teaching it. Try the link method yourself. While this technique is easier for children and adolescents to learn at first, most adults can also learn to use it with practice.

While most students in middle grades will be able to visualize or see mental images, a few may not. Do not suggest this possibility at the beginning of the lesson, as the suggestion may negatively influence students' efforts. Rather, be prepared for the possibility that some students in a class may experience an inability to see mental images. Explain to students that most people can learn to visualize more clearly through practice.

STUDENT TEXT

A Memory Game

Directions: In this game, you'll find six different groups of letters. They are lined up in different ways to make it easier for you to concentrate on one group at a time.

(continued)

Read over group 1 below. Then cover it with your hand. How many of the letters can you remember? Write all the letters from group 1 that you can remember on the line below that group. Repeat for groups 2–6.

6. g   t   j
   x   k   r   d
   n   a   q   l
   i   c

1. d   h   r   c   w   j   v

_____

_____

3. f   m   z   u   g   w   k   s   a   p   n   r   l

_____

2. r   l   s
   v   q   i
   x   a   g

5. a   b   c   d   l   m   n   o   v   w   x   y   z

_____

_____

_____

4. t   k   q   d   y   a   f

_____

Suggested Directions for Unit VII

1. Read the directions for "A Memory Game" aloud. Ask students to follow the directions individually. When they have done so, discuss the results of their "playing" the game. Ask questions like the following:

   • Could you remember all of the letters?

   • For which groups of letters did you struggle to remember them all?

   • What were the differences between the groups you remembered and the ones you did not?

   • Can you draw any conclusions based on these differences?

   • Was group 5 different in any way from groups 3 and 6?

   Help students to see that most people can only remember up to nine pieces of information at any moment. And grouping or chunking letters or numbers into segments improves one's ability to remember strings of information (e.g., think of telephone numbers grouped in three-number then four-number formats: 555-555-1234). Also, help students explore the differences between group 5 and groups 3 and 6. Let students discover other conclusions on their own.

STUDENT TEXT

Learning about Your Memory

There are two levels of memory: short-term memory and long-term memory.

Short-term memory is what you can keep in your attention in the moment. Most people can remember only five to nine different things in their short-term memories. That is why you can remember 7 letters easily and 9 letters with a little more difficulty. Yet most people cannot remember 10 letters or more.

Long-term memory is what you know and can bring to mind whenever you choose to do so. What is in your long-term memory stays with you for a long time. If you review it now and then, you can remember it as long as you like.

You could probably remember the 13 letters in group 5 because this group contains three sequences of letters that are already part of your long-term memory: a, b, c, d, l, m, n, o, v, w, x, y, z. To remember this group, you really needed only to remember the first letter in each sequence and the length of the sequence.

---

2. Have students read "Learning about Your Memory," or have several students read it aloud. Be sure students understand the nature of short-term and long-term memory.

STUDENT TEXT

Another Memory Game

Directions: Read list A twice. Then cover the list with your hand, and write down in the blanks as many words from list A as you can recall. Next, turn the page so you can read list B. Do the same with list B as you did with list A.

List A

pharmacy	heat
spruce	bakery
gas	elm
oak	friction
office	theater
density	maple
fir	hotel
restaurant	

_____

_____

_____

_____

(*continued*)

How many words did you correctly recall?

_____

3. Ask students to do "Another Memory Game" individually. Most students will remember more words from list B than from list A. When they have finished the game, engage them in exploring the differences between the two lists and how this might affect memory.

STUDENT TEXT

List B

Birds	Places to Play Sports	Scientific Terms
robin	gym	orbit
sparrow	park	force
hawk	rink	conservation
eagle	pool	phase
crow	field	element

_____

_____

_____

_____

_____

How many words did you correctly recall?

_____

Ways to Remember

This unit will show you four different ways to remember: grouping, visualizing, repeating, and choosing to remember. Each of these ways can help you to "move" information *from short-term memory into long-term memory.*

(continued)

Ways to Remember: Grouping

In "Another Memory Game," you were probably able to remember more of the words in list B than in list A. The words in list A were not in any order. The words in list B were organized into three groups.

When information is grouped, it is easier to remember. Grouping means to organize information so that details are brought together under the main idea or category that connects them. For example, in "Another Memory Game," each column in list B includes five words that are examples of the category listed in the heading.

Grouping information is one way of helping to "move" it from short-term to long-term memory. When you want to remember ideas and information, try to organize them into groups that make sense to you. For example, put details with main ideas that they support. List examples with categories that they illustrate. When you group ideas and facts together, remembering one will help you to recall the others.

4. Have students read "Ways to Remember," or read it aloud. Discuss briefly. Then ask students to read "Ways to Remember: Grouping," or read it aloud. Discuss for emphasis. Then organize students into small groups of 3–4 members. Ask students to complete Exercise I.

STUDENT TEXT

Exercise I

Directions: Think about information that you need to learn and remember for this class that can be grouped in some way.

Write the names of two groups of such information on the top line in the space provided. Then list at least four details or examples for each group.

Group #1:	Group #2:

Ways to Remember: Visualizing

Visualizing means to see an image or picture in your mind's eye. For example, close your eyes right now, and visualize a mental picture of the room where you are sitting. Try this just for a few seconds. When you see this mental picture, you are visualizing.

Practice visualizing again. Close your eyes, and see the face of a friend of yours. Notice how clearly you can see the details of her or his face.

(continued)

One way to use visualizing is to see a mental picture for each main idea that you want to remember. When you want to remember something, visualize a picture of it in your mind. For many people, a mental picture is easier to remember than words are. See as clear an image as you can, and examine it for a few seconds. Then let it disappear.

Some people don't visualize clearly. If you don't, you can learn to visualize more clearly by practicing. Look at an object or a picture with your eyes. Then close your eyes and try to visualize it. The more you practice, the clearer your mental pictures will become.

Draw a picture in the space provided of something you visualized in your mind.

Did the picture you drew of what you visualized help you remember better? Why or why not?

_____

_____

_____

_____

5. Have several students read "Ways to Remember: Visualizing" aloud. Give students the opportunity to practice visualizing. Discuss for emphasis.

STUDENT TEXT

Ways to Remember: Repeating

Another good way to remember is to repeat information you want to learn. Be sure to say it in your own words. Even though you have already learned something, go over it one more time. When you repeat information in this way, it will help you move it into your long-term memory and will keep the information available to you.

One good way to repeat information is to say it aloud to yourself. When you say it aloud, not only do you speak the information, but you also hear it.

Ways to Remember: Choosing to Remember

You can always remember more effectively when you choose to remember. The more you want to learn and know, the more you will be able to remember what you have learned.

To choose to remember, you need to pay attention to and be interested in what you are learning.

6. Read "Ways to Remember: Repeating" aloud. Ask students to suggest ways they can use this method to help them learn material in class. Then read "Ways to Remember: Choosing to Remember." Ask students to share their reactions to this suggestion.

STUDENT TEXT

Mnemonics

Mnemonic methods are ways of remembering more efficiently. Two mnemonic methods are acronyms and acrostics.

Acronyms

An acronym is a word that is made by taking the first letter from each word that you want to remember and making a new word from all of those letters.

Exercise II

Directions: Try to create acronyms for remembering the two groups of information that follow. Write each acronym on the line below the information that it represents.

1. The Great Lakes: Superior, Huron, Michigan, Erie, Ontario.

   Hint: you can put the names of the lakes in any helpful order.

   Answers may vary. _____

   _____

2. The colors of visible light in the spectrum and the order in which they appear: red, orange, yellow, green, blue, indigo, violet.

   Hint: an acronym can be more than one word.

   Answers may vary. _____

   _____

Exercise III

Directions: Can you create any acronyms that can help you remember information that you need to know? List any acronyms that you can create in the space provided.

_____

_____

_____

_____

_____

---

7. Have students read "Mnemonics" and "Acronyms," or have several students read these aloud. Discuss as needed. Then have students do Exercise II in pairs. When they have finished, go over the exercise. Follow the same procedure for Exercise III.

STUDENT TEXT

Acrostics

An acrostic is a sentence that is made by taking the first letter from each word or symbol that you want to remember and then inserting another word beginning with the same letter. For example, to help you remember the lines on a musical staff, the acrostic is: <u>E</u>very <u>G</u>ood <u>B</u>oy <u>D</u>oes <u>F</u>ine.

E—Every

G—Good

B—Boy

D—Does

F—Fine

Another useful acrostic can help you remember the classification system of living things in biology: King Phillip came over for green stamps.

Kingdom—K—King

Phylum—P—Phillip

Class—C—came

Order—O—over

Family—F—for

Genus—G—green

Species—S—stamps

(continued)

80

Do you know any acrostics that have been useful to you?

_____

_____

_____

Other Mnemonic Methods

There are many other mnemonic methods, and they include methods for remembering names and numbers, errands and appointments, and other kinds of information.

If you want to learn more about mnemonic methods, there are many exercises found online and many books in the school or public library. All you need to do is practice!

8. Have students read "Acrostics" and "Other Mnemonic Methods." Give students an opportunity to share any other acrostics that they know with the class.

Additional Suggestions

1. Creating mapping notes and learning them through visualization is a memory skill that offers much value to students who visualize clearly. Help students practice this skill in relation to the notes they create. Additional examples can be found with an online search of the words "mapping notes." Or, have students design their own mapping notes.

STUDENT TEXT

Unit VII Summary

- There are two levels of memory: short-term memory and long-term memory.

- Short-term memory is what you can keep in your attention in the moment. Most people can only remember five to nine different things in their short-term memories.

- Long-term memory is what you know and can bring to mind whenever you choose to do so.

- An important part of learning is "moving" information from your short-term memory into your long-term memory. Four ways to accomplish this are:

  o Grouping information: To group information is to organize it so that details are brought together under the main idea or category that connects them.

(continued)

---

     o Visualizing information: To visualize information is to see an image or picture of it in your mind's eye.

     o Repeating information: To repeat information is to put the information in your own words and go over it. Say it aloud to yourself so you can hear it as well as speak it.

     o Choosing to remember: The more you choose to remember, the more you will remember. To choose to remember, you need to want to pay attention to and be interested in what you are learning.

- Mnemonics is the art of remembering. Mnemonic methods are ways of remembering more efficiently. Two useful mnemonics methods are:

     o Acronym: An acronym is a word that is made by taking the first letter from each word you want to remember and making a new word from all of those letters.

     o Acrostic: An acrostic is a sentence that is made by taking the first letter from each word or symbol you want to remember and inserting another word beginning with that same letter.

Suggested Retrieval Activities

As part of closure and retrieval of information learned, ask students to do one or more of the following:

- Have students use one of the memory methods discussed in this unit to prepare for a test in another class. Allow students time to prepare and present a brief presentation of their work so other students (who may be taking the same test in the other class) can benefit from their memory technique.

- Prepare a list of items you want students to memorize (e.g., sports teams [city and team name], states and state capitals, or U.S. president and vice president names). Have students take a pretest using these items and see how they score. Then, encourage students to use a memory technique they have learned (either one presented in this unit or a memory technique they found on their own) and allow them time to implement the technique and practice it for the list of items you prepared earlier. Give a posttest and chart the results. Determine what progress was made, and if one method was better than another.

STUDENT TEXT

Technology Adaptation

- Search online for memory exercises or memory games. Prepare a multimedia presentation to demonstrate to others how to use the method you discovered.

- Produce a diagram using mapping notes. You can also use free websites to list your ideas and create the diagram automatically. Some examples include:

(continued)

- spidescribe.net—allows users to easily visualize their ideas by connecting various pieces of information together. The site also combines elements like text, images, and other files.

- editstorm—allows users to work on ideas and organize them into sticky notes for others to see.

- bubbl.us—great site for mind-mapping and brainstorming. It allows users to create concept maps easily and with minimal tools. You can invite others to join in as editors to your mind map.

UNIT VIII
ORGANIZING IDEAS

The skills involved in organizing ideas and information are among the most critical taught in school. Many students at this age have difficulty organizing a hierarchy of ideas. It is often hard for them to label and use topics, main ideas, and supporting details. Student should start with practical or relevant applications of the concepts of main ideas and supporting details, such as how items of clothing might be organized in a drawer. Once the student understands this kind of application, he or she is more able to pursue abstract applications.

Exercises I and II are designed to help students increase their understanding of the relationship between main ideas and supporting details. These activities also give them practice in determining which is which. Students are presented with the information in several ways:

1. with the main ideas and details highlighted

2. with just the main ideas highlighted

3. with just the details highlighted

4. with neither highlighted but both contained within the situation

Students need to sort through the ways the information in each situation is presented so they can generate usable lists.

Exercises III and IV introduce the concept of topic. Exercise V asks the students to integrate all of these ideas and gain a sense of the relationship among them. Consider this unit carefully before beginning. Decide if tackling these activities would be best suited for students working small groups, in pairs, or individually.

If you have students with little experience in these skills, working with group lessons may be the best approach. It is also important to practice exercises that provide individual practice. There are suggestions for further practice in the "Additional Suggestions" section of this unit.

STUDENT TEXT

Introduction

The unit "Putting Ideas Together" presented how organizing ideas and information into categories can improve memory. This skill is useful in many other ways. For example, you can find clothes in a drawer more easily if each drawer holds a certain category or type of clothes. You can find information in a school notebook more efficiently if there are categories or sections. You would even find cooking an easier task if like ingredients are stored in categories or on certain shelves in the kitchen.

When you organize ideas and information into categories, the name of each category you create is a main idea. Each idea or piece of information in the category is a detail. In the shopping list below, the main ideas are at the top of each list of details.

Example Situation

You have to go shopping, and you only have a certain amount of time. You have to find the things on your list quickly. So you organize your list into the sections of the grocery store:

Dairy	Baking Goods	Produce	Frozen Foods
milk	baking soda	oranges	ice cream
eggs	chocolate chips	celery	microwavable dinner
yogurt	yeast	lettuce	frozen corn
butter	brown sugar	carrots	
cheese	flour	radishes	
	baking powder	spinach	
		apples	

Suggested Directions for Unit VIII

1. Read over the introduction with students. Go over the example situation. Ask the following questions:

   • What is the difference between a main idea and a detail?

   • How can this list help you find groceries in a busy store?

   • Do you have any personal systems in which you use a type of category or main idea to organize details?

STUDENT TEXT

Exercise I

Directions: Read the following situations. Each situation requires you to make a list so that you can do the work more efficiently.

Make a list that has main ideas for headings. Place the details below the correct main ideas. Your lists should look something like the shopping list on the "Example Situation." Please feel free to shorten the details into notes.

Situation A

You have a test for science class tomorrow on animal characteristics. You are required to know the characteristics of amphibians, mammals, and birds.

You must know which of the characteristics below fits with what kind of animal:

- feeds young with mammary glands

- lives in water and on land

- has wings

- reproduces by laying eggs

- reproduces by giving birth to young animal

- has hair

- has gill-breathing larvae

- has hollow bones

- has backbones

- has feathers

- has gelatinous eggs

(*continued*)

First write your main ideas. Then organize the list of details in the spaces below. You may use a detail more than once.

Main Ideas:	_Amphibians_	_Mammals_	_Birds_
Details:	_lives in water and on land_	_feeds young with mammary glands_	_has wings_
	reproduces by laying eggs	_reproduces by giving birth to young animal_	_has backbones_
	has backbones	_has backbones_	_has feathers_
	has gill-breathing larvae	_has hair_	_has hollow bones_
	has gelatinous eggs		

2. Read the directions to Exercise I together. Do situation A as a whole class. As you do this exercise, point out how the details can be shortened into notes. Note that the lists are much easier to read and use than paragraphs.

STUDENT TEXT
Situation B

You have to write a biography about a famous person. You have to answer these questions about the person:

1. What happened in the person's early years?

2. What kind of education did the person receive?

3. What made this person famous?

You choose Abraham Lincoln because you already know the following about him: he walked three miles to school each way to get a good education; his mother was Nancy Hanks; he had one sister; his father was Thomas Lincoln; the family moved from Kentucky to Indiana when Lincoln was young; he went to school to become a lawyer; he could write well; he debated Stephen Douglass; he was a captain in the Black Hawk War; he trained as a store clerk; and he became sixteenth president of the United States.

First write your main ideas. Then organize your list. Add any other details that you know.

Main Ideas:	_Early years_	_Education_	_Fame_
Details:	_one sister_	_three miles to school_	_debated Douglass_
	Father—Thomas	_school for lawyers_	_Black Hawk War_
	Mother—Nancy	_trained as clerk_	_wrote well_
	moved KY to IN		_sixteenth president_

3. Have the students complete situation B individually. Accept any reasonable answers.

STUDENT TEXT

Exercise II

Directions: Read situation A and follow the directions at the end of the situation. Do the same for situation B.

Situation A

Before you can get this week's allowance, your parents insist that you do the following chores:

make bed each day

study for math test

put away clean clothes

mow the lawn

pick up dirty clothes

work on social studies report

load the dishwasher

feed and water the pets

read three chapters in the novel for English class

In the space provided, make lists of all the chores you have to do. Make sure each list has an appropriate main idea for a heading.

Main Ideas:	*Schoolwork*	*Housework*	*Yardwork*
Details:	*study for math test*	*make bed*	*mow lawn*
	social studies report	*put away clean clothes*	_____
	three chapters for English	*pick up dirty clothes*	_____
	_____	*load dishwasher*	_____
	_____	*feed and water pets*	_____

(continued)

Situation B

You are going on an overnight camping trip with family friends. It is your assignment to bring the following items: sleeping bag, bottled water, lantern, board game, playing cards, fruit, cereal, doughnuts, life jacket, flashlight, extra blankets, fishing gear, peanut butter and crackers, and a tarp.

In the space provided, categorize the items you are assigned to bring. Make sure each list has an appropriate main idea for a heading. Create your list in the space provided.

Main Ideas:	*Food*	*Games*	*Supplies*
Details:	*bottled water*	*board game*	*sleeping bag*
	fruit	*playing cards*	*lantern*
	cereal	_____	*life jacket*
	doughnuts	_____	*flashlight*
	peanut butter and crackers	_____	*extra blankets*
	_____	_____	*fishing gear*
	_____	_____	*tarp*

4. Have the students complete Exercise II. Accept any reasonable answers.

STUDENT TEXT

Topics

A topic is broader or larger than a main idea. It can include several main ideas.

Exercise III

Directions: Read statements 1 through 4, and answer the questions on the lines provided.

1. The topic of situation A in Exercise I might be living things or animals. Is there any other topic these ideas might fit under?

_____

(*continued*)

2. The topic of situation B in Exercise I might be presidents or famous politicians. Can you think of any other topic it could be?

_____

3. The topic of situation A in Exercise II might be chores or ways to earn money. Can you think of another topic that would fit these ideas?

_____

4. The topic of situation B in Exercise II might be scout trips or hiking plans. Can you think of another topic that would fit these ideas?

_____

5. Read aloud "Topics." Discuss for emphasis. Then have students do Exercise III. Have students share their answers. Accept any reasonable answers.

STUDENT TEXT

Exercise IV

Directions: Read the lists in #1 below. Create a topic for the main ideas and details in #1, and write it on the line provided. Do the same for #2.

1.

Food	Favors	Activities	To Do
cake	napkins	video game	get a cake
ice cream	noisemakers	outdoor sports	send invites
snacks	hats	board game	go shopping
hamburgers	prizes	contests	set up for party
rolls			bake brownies
ketchup/mustard			
brownies			

The topic is *party preparations* _____

(continued)

2.

Early Years	Education	Events Leading to Fame
one of seven	taught by older brother	became leader of Virginia militia
father died when young	no formal schooling	member of the First Continental Congress
favored son	learned surveying	General of the Continental Army
raised in Virginia	took over brother's military duties	commander at Valley Forge
took over Mount Vernon at a young age	surveyed wilderness of America	first President of the United States

The topic is *George Washington*

6. Read the directions for Exercise IV aloud. Do the exercise as a group or ask students to do each individually. Go over their answers. Accept any reasonable answers.

STUDENT TEXT

Exercise V

Directions: Pick a topic from the suggestions listed. Circle the topic. Then in the spaces provided, write out three lists showing main ideas and details that fit with this topic.

World War II	mammals	famous authors
famous women	automobiles	famous politicians
vacation spots	schools	flight
television	technology	agriculture
pets	entertainment	food
clothing	careers	twentieth century
plant kingdom	books	explorers

Main Ideas: _____ _____ _____

Details: _____ _____ _____

_____ _____ _____

_____ _____ _____

_____ _____ _____

_____ _____ _____

_____ _____ _____

_____ _____ _____

_____ _____ _____

7. Explain Exercise V, and have students complete it for homework. Collect the assignment, and give feedback about their lists. Answers may vary.

Additional Suggestions

1. Assign students a research topic such as "Famous People." As a class, generate the main ideas within the topic. Work with no more than three main ideas at a time. Utilize resources such as the library and online websites, and help them to find supporting details for their main ideas.

2. Introduce content areas by labeling the relevant topic and main ideas that students will be studying. Ask students how many supporting details they already know about each main idea. For example, say:

"We will be studying a topic called 'Communities' over the next two weeks. What can you tell me about the following?" (display for the class)

Communities

rural   city   suburbs   village   town

As students suggest details, write their suggestions under the appropriate main idea. This is also a good way to design a unit based on what students already know about a topic.

3. Cut out advertisements from newspapers and magazines. Have students place the ads into topics (food, hygiene products, recreation, etc.). Then have students identify the main idea of each ad and its supporting details. Students may even take these main ideas to create their own advertisements and supporting details.

STUDENT TEXT

Unit VIII Summary

A category name is also a main idea. The ideas and information within a category are the details of that main idea.

Details give more information about or support about a main idea.

A topic is broader or larger than a main idea. It often includes several main ideas.

DETAILS are part of MAIN IDEAS are part of a TOPIC

or

A TOPIC includes MAIN IDEAS are supported by DETAILS

Suggested Retrieval Activities

As part of closure and retrieval of information learned, ask students to do one or more of the following:

- Have students read a book of their choice (possibly for class credit). As they read their selection, ask students to look for the topic of the book, as well as main ideas and supporting details. Have student use the form they are used to using from this unit:

The topic is _____

Main Ideas: _____   _____   _____

Details: _____   _____   _____

_____   _____   _____

_____   _____   _____

_____   _____   _____

- For further scaffolding of this material, have students compare the lists about their books (once they have completed reading) and have students group with others on similar topics to create a broader topic of what they have read (what is in common). Students will then begin to see the connections between similar books. Students in groups can then support their common topics with main ideas and supporting details using text or situations from their books as examples. Students may need guidance in grouping with others to find those who have read books with similar themes or genres. Present findings to the class.

- Have students create their own topic and suggested lists like they completed in the exercises in this unit. Then, have students group together to see if others can provide the main ideas and supporting details using the form they are used to using from this unit.

The topic is _____

Main Ideas: _____   _____   _____

Details: _____   _____   _____

   _____   _____   _____

   _____   _____   _____

   _____   _____   _____

   _____   _____   _____

STUDENT TEXT

Technology Adaptation

- Create a website with other classmates or work individually to create a website. There are free website resources such as Weebly.com to create a simple website for free.

- The terms *topic*, *main idea*, and *supporting details* discussed in this unit are found in virtually every website. The "topic" of a website is usually the broad intent of what the website will offer potential users. The "main ideas" are then major subcategories based on the overall topic, while the "supporting details" are simply data. An example would be for you and your classmates to create a website for organizing a talent show in your school. "Talent show" would be the topic, and main ideas might include: community event, fund-raiser, building school culture and tradition, and having fun. Supporting details (or data) would be where and when the show will be held, how auditions are conducted, what prizes are awarded, how much tickets will cost, and so on. Present your website to the class. If the topic of the website is school related (such as the talent show example) consider asking school officials if the project could be conducted.

- Create a website for: keeping statistics about the local weather, creating a book list and allowing for blogs or reviews for those books online, and planning a community service event.

- Create a form using an application like Google Docs. In the form, create your own topic and suggested lists like you completed in the exercises in this unit. Then share the form with other classmates and see if others can provide the main ideas and supporting details for your topic.

- Create a PowerPoint or Prezi to present a class report by selecting a topic that interests you and presenting main ideas and supporting details on the topic. This is a "show and tell"–type exercise using technology.

UNIT IX
READING FOR MEANING

This unit focuses on reading a textbook, taking notes from reading, and taking notes from listening. As the foundation skills involved in these tasks are much the same, this can be seen as part of a whole.

When faced with a reading assignment in a text, most students in the middle school years begin with the first word in the assignment and continue as far as their interest, sense of duty, or fear of failure carries them. Yet regardless of how far they get in their reading, the method used is the same ineffective one because the reading is done without thought or purpose.

This unit introduces the students to a way of reading texts that can be much more effective for learning than starting with the first word and reading as far as one gets. The method is *reading for meaning*, and it includes four steps: surveying, reading, mapping, and checking yourself.

Integrated with the *reading for meaning* method are several important concepts and skills. Students are probably familiar with some of these and unfamiliar with others. While these skills and concepts can be taught separately, we have presented them in an integrated way in this unit because this is the way a student would actually use them.

The skills and concepts are the following:

1. *Understanding what main ideas and supporting details are and locating them in a paragraph or passage*

This is a key thinking skill with which the students may need additional work. Several useful sources for teaching main ideas and supporting details are listed in the "Additional Suggestions" in this unit.

2. *Recognizing the topic sentence of a paragraph*

Some students will probably be familiar with this skill but may need review. Others may require more specific instruction. Give all students practice in locating topic sentences in the beginning, middle, and end of paragraphs. Examine paragraphs that don't state the topic sentence at all. A good way to have the students review this skill further is to have them write sample paragraphs.

3. *Surveying*

Students may already know about a related skill called *scanning*. Introduce them to *surveying* by comparing it with *scanning*. Another introductory exercise is this: hand the students various paperback books and ask them, "Which of these books do you think you'd like to read?" They'll probably "survey" the books by checking the titles, number of pages, size of print, kinds of illustrations, and so on. Perhaps they will read a little of the texts. When students have finished "surveying," discuss with them what they have done to examine the books and what they have learned.

4. *Mapping*

Mapping is a pictorial method of taking notes. As students of middle school age are highly tactually and visually oriented, they can often work with ideas more effectively through pictorial or visual representations. Such representations also help them to retain the ideas.

Mapping is an alternative method that can prove extremely useful to students for whom pictorial representations of ideas and information are easier to create, manipulate, and recall than linear representations, such as outlining. Mapping is also very useful in situations where the presentation lacks a clear sense of organization, such as class discussions.

5. *Checking yourself*

When students first try this step, they often gain more by telling what they know to each other, or, when possible, to an older student or an adult. As they speak, they often discover the gaps in their understanding of what they have read. As students become more confident about this step, they are more likely to use self-recitation effectively.

Give students practice with this step by having them "check themselves" with peers. Encourage them to use this step by talking with their parents and older siblings.

We offer two alternatives for teaching this unit. Read through alternatives carefully to choose the one best suited for your class.

The first alternative is best suited to a group of students who have already had some exposure to "reading for meaning." In this alternative, take several class periods to introduce the concepts separately. Put them all together by teaching the "reading for meaning" method, using the content from the curriculum.

A Note about Teaching Methods

The usefulness to any student of the "reading for meaning" method clearly depends on his or her ability to use the method individually. For the purpose of introducing students to this method, organize the class into small groups, as noted in the directions. Many students will find the "reading for meaning" method detailed and challenging. Students working in groups will be more willing to become engaged in learning the various steps of the method as a result of their participation in a group.

Encourage students to share the work of the group actively, even if it seems inefficient at times. Then, after the initial lesson, structure assignments that will require the student to use the "reading for meaning" method on an individual basis.

STUDENT TEXT

How Do You Read?

"Read the assignment in your book, and be ready for a quiz!"

This is a direction you probably often hear in school. When you are given this direction, what do you do?

Look at the reading "The Race to the Moon" in this unit. If your teacher asked you to read this and be ready for a quiz about it, what would you do? On the lines below, briefly describe *how* you would complete this assignment.

Remember: Don't actually read the section now. Just describe each step you would use and *how* you would read it.

_____

_____

_____

_____

_____

Suggested Directions for Unit IX

Class Period I

1. Read "How Do You Read?" aloud to the students. If necessary, briefly clarify the assignment. Then tell students they will have two minutes to complete the assignment. When they are done, have several students read aloud what they have written. See if others have different responses. Discuss briefly. Then read the introduction aloud to students, or have a student read it aloud.

2. Divide the class into small groups of two or three members. Have students work all of the exercises in these groups.

STUDENT TEXT

The Race to the Moon

Sputnik Launched!

On October 4, 1957, the U.S.S.R. astounded the American public by launching Sputnik I. Sputnik I was the first man-made satellite to orbit the earth. On November 3rd of the same year, the Soviets sent another Sputnik, Sputnik II, into orbit, carrying a dog named Laika. The race to the moon was on.

(continued)

The United States Responds

The United States was caught off guard by the advanced technology of the Soviet space program. In the year following the launching of Sputnik I, the U.S. Congress authorized billions of dollars to be put into an American space program. NASA, the National Aeronautics and Space Administration, was created in 1958. In that same year the United States launched its first satellite, Explorer I.

The First Travelers in Space

A few years later the Soviet Union sent the first traveler into outer space. On April 7, 1961, Yuri Gagarin became the first man to journey into the farthest reaches of the Earth's atmosphere. In 1963 Valentina Tereshkova became the first woman to fly into outer space.

The First American Astronaut

In the years between 1961 and 1963 the American space program was also busy. The United States launched its first manned flight in May 1961. Alan Shepherd rode a tiny capsule that was launched from Cape Canaveral in Florida. Shepherd's flight lasted only fifteen minutes. Americans huddled around their TV sets to watch the launch. Telstar, the first communications satellite, was also launched in 1961.

Amazing Breakthroughs in 1965

Amazing breakthroughs engineered by both countries took place in 1965. Leonov of the U.S.S.R. made the first space walk from the Voshkod spacecraft. The United States launched the first of the Gemini space flights, each of which orbited the Earth many times. Luna 9 of the U.S.S.R. and Surveyor I of the United States were both unmanned spacecraft that made soft landings on the moon during this year. A Soviet probe crash-landed on Venus. And the United States' Mariner 4 transmitted the first close-up pictures of Mars over a distance of 217 million kilometers.

Orbiting the Moon

After many different kinds of space experiments had been conducted by both nations, the United States made a great thrust to the moon in 1968. The American astronauts Frank Borman, William Anders, and James Lovell Jr. orbited the moon ten times on December 24–25 of that year.

Moon Landing!

Finally in July 1969 American astronauts Armstrong and Aldrin placed their feet on the surface of the moon. The race between nations was over. The plaque the astronauts left on the moon said: "Here men from Earth first set forth on the moon. July 1969 A.D. We came in peace for all mankind."

Introduction

Many students don't have a special way of reading a textbook. They may start with the first word in the assignment and read as far as they get. Unfortunately, this isn't a very good way to learn from reading.

This unit will show you a way of reading an assignment in a textbook and learning from what was read. This method is called *reading for meaning*. You may find that this method is new to you and will take a little more time at first. You might also find it a little tricky. Stay with it! Learn how to use this method, and you will become a better learner.

Remember, the goal for reading is not to just finish; the goal is to *understand* after you have finished the text.

(*continued*)

Reading for Meaning

When you read a paragraph or section in your textbook, what you really want to find out is:

What is the *main idea* of this reading?

What are the *important details* that support the *main idea?*

Reading for meaning means locating *main ideas* and the *supporting details* in your reading.

Another way to think of *reading for meaning* is this: when you read for meaning, you're trying to find out what the paragraph or section is trying to tell you. Ask yourself these questions:

What does the person who wrote this paragraph or section want me to know?

What is this paragraph or section trying to tell me?

3. Read aloud "Reading for Meaning," or have a student read it aloud. Discuss briefly for emphasis. Then have students do Exercise I. Go over the exercise.

STUDENT TEXT

Exercise I

Directions: Read the paragraph below. Then write the main idea of the paragraph on the lines that follow.

Remember: The *main idea* in a paragraph is the most important idea. The *main idea* is the idea that the writer is trying to share with you.

Paragraph A

Dogs have a very powerful sense of smell that they can use to find things. Police use tracking dogs to search for people who are missing in the woods. The dogs sniff a piece of clothing owned by the missing person. Then they try to track the scent in the area where the person was last seen. Often these dogs can find people who are lost when the police have no other way of locating them. Another kind of tracking dog is the hunting hound. These dogs can follow animals for miles through the forest once they have sniffed their scent. Though some dogs are better than others in using their sense of smell, all dogs have a stronger sense of smell than people do.

Main idea: *Dogs have a strong sense of smell and can use it for tracking.*

_____

_____

_____

_____

(*continued*)

Main Idea and Supporting Details

We know that the *main idea* of a paragraph is the most important idea in that paragraph.

Most paragraphs also have *supporting details.* Supporting details explain, prove, or tell something about the main idea of the paragraph. They make the main idea more clear to us or give us more information about it.

These details are called *supporting* details because they "hold up" the main idea. This means that they give us reasons to believe the main idea and help us to understand it.

Exercise II

Directions: Read paragraph A again. On the lines that follow, list *three* supporting details for the main idea.

1. *Tracking by smell, dogs can find people who are lost in the woods.*

2. *Dogs can track prey for hunters.*

3. *Some dogs are better than others at tracking by smell.*

4. Have a student read aloud "Main Idea and Supporting Details," or read it aloud to them. Have students do Exercise II. Go over the exercise.

STUDENT TEXT

Exercise III

Directions: Find the main idea for the paragraph that follows. Then locate two supporting details. Write the main idea and supporting details on the appropriate lines. Do the same for paragraphs C and D.

Paragraph B

In the early days America was a country full of individuals who did many things well. One man stands out from all the rest. This man helped to organize many institutions in the new country: the U.S. Post Office; the Pennsylvania Academy; Pennsylvania Hospital, the first in America. He also organized the first American expedition to the Arctic region. He was an inventor, inventing many useful things including the Franklin stove, the lightning rod, bifocal glasses, and an instrument he called the "Armonica." He also wrote books and newspapers and took part in the politics of early America. Benjamin Franklin was a man of many talents.

Main idea: *Ben Franklin was a man of many talents.*

(continued)

Supporting details:

1. _Ben Franklin organized many institutions._

2. _He organized the first American expedition to the Arctic._

3. _He invented many useful things._

4. _He wrote books and newspapers._

5. _He took part in the politics of early America._

Paragraph C

She was an adult female who died three million years ago. The archaeologists who found her bones nicknamed her "Lucy." They did not find her entire skeleton. However, a description of Lucy can be based on the bones they found. She was a Hominidae, a primate that stood and walked on two legs. She had a skeleton much like ours. But she was tiny compared to today's humans. She stood three feet, eight inches tall and weighed about 65 pounds. Her thick bones show that she must have had great muscular strength. Lucy's face and apelike jutting jaws were large, but her brain was probably only one-third the size of a modern human's.

Main idea: _"Lucy" can be described from the bones they found._

Supporting details:

1. _Lucy was a Hominidae._

2. _She had a skeleton much like ours._

3. _She stood three feet, eight inches and weighed 65 pounds._

4. _She had great muscular strength._

5. _She had a large, apelike face._

6. _She had a small brain._

Paragraph D

The man lowered a hydrophone into the water. This phone was meant to pick up the clicks, whistles, and short piercing screams of the killer whales. He explained that the clicks seem to be a way that the whales tell each other where food is located. The whistles are heard most often between resting or socializing whales. But, he explained, the most interesting of all are the screams. They are different within each whale pod (a pod is a group of whales). This suggests that whales are among the few animals that have a local dialect or a special way of speaking to the others that live in the same region.

(_continued_)

Main idea: *Killer whales communicate with each other.*

Supporting details:

1. *The whales use clicks to tell where food is located.*

2. *The whales use whistles for socializing.*

3. *Whales have different screams within each pod.*

4. *Whales may have a dialect.*

5. Have the students read "How Do You Find the Main Idea?" Discuss for clarity and emphasis.

6. Have students work through "How to Read for Meaning." Lead them through each step of the reading for meaning method.

7. Complete Exercise IV and V. For Exercise IV, be sure to give students only one minute to survey the paragraph. Then ask them to write the main idea.

STUDENT TEXT

How Do You Find the Main Idea?

The main idea of a paragraph is stated in the *topic sentence.* The purpose of the *topic sentence* is to tell you the main idea. For example, in the paragraph about the strong sense of smell that dogs have, the topic sentence is the first one.

When you read a paragraph, the main idea will sometimes be very clear to you. When it's not clear, use these hints for finding it:

1. Most often the topic sentence is the first sentence in the paragraph. This means that you'll often find the main idea in the first sentence of a paragraph.

2. Sometimes the topic sentence is the last sentence in a paragraph. When the first sentence doesn't tell you the main idea, look at the last sentence in the paragraph and see if it's there.

3. In some paragraphs, the topic sentence is in the middle of the paragraph. In these paragraphs, you can only find the main idea by reading the paragraph carefully and figuring out what the paragraph is telling you.

4. In some paragraphs, there is no topic sentence. The main idea is not stated clearly in any one sentence of the paragraph. Often this happens when the main idea has already been stated in another paragraph. When this happens, you really have to read carefully to see if you can figure out what the paragraph is trying to tell you.

(continued)

How to Read for Meaning

Reading for meaning means finding the main idea and supporting details in your reading. You can read for meaning by using these four steps:

- surveying

- reading

- mapping

- checking yourself

Step 1: Surveying

When you first start to read a paragraph, don't read it word for word. Instead *survey* the paragraph first.

Surveying means to look quickly at any heading or titles over the paragraph and then read the first and last sentences. *Surveying* will usually let you find out what the paragraph's main idea is. And it takes only a minute or less!

Exercise IV

Directions: Survey the paragraph that follows. On the lines below it, write what you think the *main idea* of this paragraph is.

A Profit in Frogs

People don't usually think of frog raising as a profitable business, but many people are willing to pay for frogs. Universities and high schools buy frogs for use in their science labs. Restaurants will pay $4.50 or more for a pound of dressed frog meat, as frogs are considered a delicacy by many people. NASA uses frogs in space and will pay $25 or more for a healthy bullfrog. Probably more frogs have orbited the earth than people. People who own ponds will also buy frogs because frogs can help to keep down the insect population. So, the next time you think about leaving a frog in your teacher's desk, you may decide that there's a more profitable use for your hopping, green friend.

People will buy frogs. _____

_____

_____

_____

Step 2: Reading

Once you've *surveyed* a paragraph, you usually have a sense of what the *main idea* is. Now *read* the paragraph at your normal rate of reading. As you *read*, look for *supporting details* that prove, explain, or tell you more about the main idea.

(continued)

Exercise V

Directions: Read the paragraph about "A Profit in Frogs." As you read, be sure to look for supporting details. List at least two details on the lines below.

1. *Universities and high schools buy frogs for science labs.*

2. *Restaurants buy frogs for food.*

3. *NASA uses frogs for space experiments.*

4. *People buy frogs to help with insect control.*

Step 3: Mapping

Mapping is a way of taking notes about your reading. Look at the *map* below for the paragraph about frogs.

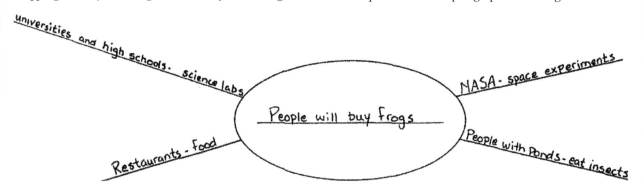

You can take *mapping* notes in this way:

1. First, write the *main idea* on a line in the middle of your paper. Then circle the *main idea*.

2. Write each *supporting detail* you find on a line that touches the circle around the *main idea*.

Mapping is a way of taking notes that helps you to understand what the main idea is and what the supporting details are.

Exercise VI

Directions: Survey the paragraph below. Then read it and take notes in the *map* below the paragraph.

Smart Chimps!

Chimpanzees are among the most intelligent animals on earth other than human beings. The structure or makeup of the chimpanzee brain is a lot like the structure of the human brain. Chimps have the ability to use simple tools. In recent years, scientists have found that chimps communicate with each other through noises and gestures. Chimps also seem to be able to learn words and make signs that stand for words.

(continued)

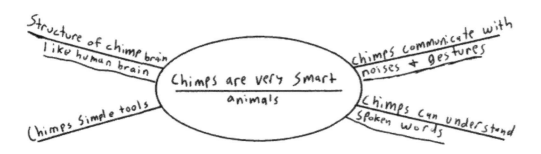

Step 4: Checking Yourself

Now, look at your mapping notes and *check yourself*. Using only your notes, tell yourself what you learned. Or tell someone who hasn't read the paragraph.

When you take a little time to *check yourself*, you'll see what you have learned. And you'll find it much easier to remember what you have read.

Exercise VII

Directions: Go back and look through the four steps. They are surveying, reading, mapping, and checking yourself.

Then use the four steps to *read for meaning* the following three paragraphs.

Visitors from Outer Space

You may not believe in extraterrestrial life forms, but the fact is that we get "visitors" from outer space daily. Each year at least 20,000 tons of material from meteors enters our atmosphere. This means about 50 tons a day! Chances of the meteors being big enough to cause us any harm are incredibly slim. The earth's atmosphere burns up the material from outer space before it can reach the surface of the earth. Only 10 to 20 new meteors are actually found on the earth's surface each year. But as they enter the earth's atmosphere, the burning can be seen from earth as a streak of light. So, we should be able to locate a "falling star" on any clear night.

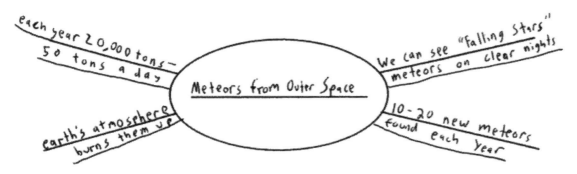

The World Has Been Round for a Long Time!

Some say that Columbus discovered that the world was round. This is not entirely true. Many people knew the world was round long before the days of Columbus. The Greek mathematician Pythagoras declared that the world was round in the

(continued)

sixth century B.C. A few hundred years later, the Greek scholar Eratosthenes figured the distance around the world. During the same time period, Aristotle reported rumors of lands on the other side of the globe. The Greek mapmaker Strabo wrote of men's attempts to sail around the world in the seventh century A.D. Many well-educated men of Columbus's day agreed with Columbus that it was perfectly possible to reach the east by sailing west because the earth was a sphere. So, you see, the idea that the earth is round has been around for a long time.

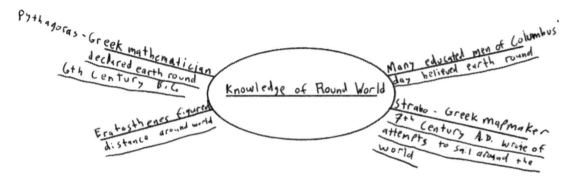

The Gentle Ape

It's hard to imagine any relative of King Kong as being gentle. But according to Dr. Francine Paterson, the 230-pound Koko is just that. Koko is a lowland female gorilla who has been working with Dr. Paterson for over a decade. By the use of sign language, Koko let Dr. Paterson know that she wanted a kitten for her birthday. When Paterson gave her a little kitten, Koko was delighted. She spent many hours playing with the tiny animal, carrying her kitten from place to place, gently stroking its fur, and bending over to give it a kiss. When the kitten died, Koko was struck with deep grief. It wasn't until the kitten was replaced that Koko resumed her normal activities. It might also interest you to know that Koko is a vegetarian. She obviously prefers petting small creatures to eating them!

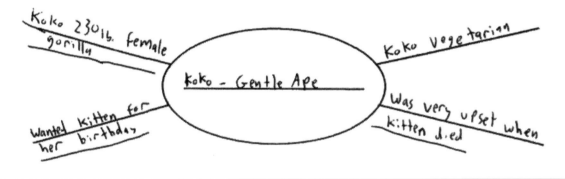

Additional Suggestions

1. You can create activities that require students to read for main ideas:

   a. Cut out interesting newspaper articles without the headlines; ask your students to create headlines for these articles.

   b. Cut out newspaper articles and their headlines. Put the articles in one box and the headlines in another. Ask students to match the articles with their headlines.

   c. Have students create ads for certain products. Tell them that they must write and design the ads so that the most useful aspects of the product are stressed.

   d. Have students view a short segment of *Sesame Street*. Tell them beforehand they are going to be looking for the teaching or main idea behind each skit, so they don't think they are being asked to do a childish task. Discuss the main ideas and how they were illustrated.

2. Give students topic sentences that summarize parts of a lesson or a unit taught. Ask students to state the main ideas expressed in the topic sentences and supply the supporting details in mapping form. Students can do this kind of exercise individually or in groups.

3. Give students practice in paraphrasing main ideas. You can do this in the following ways:

   a. Examine topic sentences of paragraphs. (You can use the paragraphs from this unit.) Have the students rewrite the topic sentences without changing the meaning. For example, "Killer whales communicate with each other" could be rewritten as "Killer whales send messages to other killer whales."

   b. Have students retitle headlines, article titles, or chapter headings.

   c. Give students paragraphs at a higher reading level with the topic sentences underlined. Have the students rewrite these topic sentences "in their own words."

4. Review Unit I. Do the same kind of activity as the one in this unit, but ask students to listen for main ideas and supporting details. Make a game of this by offering so many points for a correctly stated main idea and points for details.

Suggested Retrieval Activities

As part of closure and retrieval of information learned, ask students to do one or more of the following:

- Write a summary paragraph about what was learned today.

- Pretend a classmate was absent and write a note explaining what he/she missed.

- Tell the person next to you three things learned today that will help you get better grades.

STUDENT TEXT

Unit IX Summary

Reading for meaning means locating *main ideas* and the important *supporting details* in your reading.

The *main idea* in a paragraph is the most important idea. It is the idea that the rest of the paragraph is about.

Supporting details explain, prove, or tell something more about the main idea. They make the main idea more clear or give more information about it.

The main idea of a paragraph is often stated in the *topic sentence*. Most often the topic sentence is the first sentence in the paragraph. It can also be the last sentence or in the middle of the paragraph.

How do you *read for meaning*? Use these four steps:

1. Surveying: Look quickly at any headings or titles above the paragraph. Then read the first and last sentences of the paragraph. Surveying will usually help you find out what the *main idea* is.

2. Reading: Read the paragraph at your normal rate of reading. As you read, look for *supporting details*.

3. Mapping: Make a map like the one that follows to take notes from your reading. Mapping helps you to learn the *main idea* and *supporting details* of the reading. It also gives you a record of the reading that you can use later.

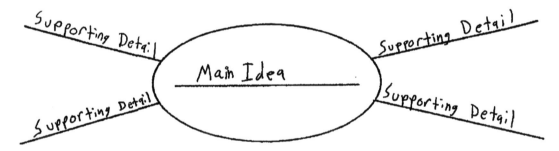

4. Checking yourself: Look at your mapping notes and tell yourself what the reading is about. Or ask yourself: What have I learned from reading this?

Technology Adaptation

*   Work with a partner to create a Google Doc. Skim back over the unit and list the most useful information.

*   Find an article online that is interesting and engaging to you. Practice skimming it to find the main idea. Next, make a list of the supporting details. Explain what was read to a classmate who is unfamiliar with the topic.

*   Make an electronic graphic organizer. Read a section of the text and complete the organizer electronically.

READING ONLINE AND USING ONLINE TEXTS

Reading and using online texts from traditional print mediums versus online formats presents many different challenges for learners. Although the technology and the Internet has made many electronic books, research databases, journals, blogs, and other sources widely available through electronic retrieval, determining what is useful and even reliable information can be difficult. Further, actually reading online poses its own set of challenges. The art of actually reading digital text may seem appealing, but the value of using a book for seeking information and learning still has a valid place in the education arena. Reading from digital text requires a degree of self control to remain focused on the topic and not distracted by other application or web pages.

In our fast-paced world, the Internet delivers quick and easy access to information. Most basic-level researchers perform a simple surface-level search of the Internet, read the information retrieved (for pleasure or for research), and then consider that information "good enough" and move on. While this may be suitable, it often does not provide the depth and breadth required for quality learning. Students must be given an opportunity to understand what is available, how to properly search, how to determine what is and what is not a good web source, and finally determine how to "weed out" bad information.

Researching, reading, and using online texts can be a beneficial for learning activities. Online texts must be approached with common sense, deciphering skills (for knowing how to utilize reliable information and removing poor information), and strong readability.

STUDENT TEXT

Introduction

In our fast-paced world, the Internet delivers quick and easy access to information. The art of actually reading digital text may seem appealing and what many more of us do now, but the value of using a book for seeking information and learning still has a valid place for students. Reading and using texts from traditional print mediums versus online formats presents many different challenges for learners. Although the technology and the Internet has made many electronic books, research databases, journals, blogs, and other sources widely available through electronic retrieval, deciphering what is useful and even reliable information can be difficult. Further, actually reading online poses its own set of challenges.

Reading from digital text requires a degree of self control to remain focused on the topic and not distracted by other application or web pages. Most basic-level researchers perform a simple surface-level search of the Internet, read the

(*continued*)

information retrieved (for pleasure or for research), and then consider that information "good enough" and move on. While this may be suitable, it often does not provide the depth and breadth required for quality learning. In these exercises, you will be given an opportunity to understand what is available online, how to properly search, how to determine what is and what is not a good web source, and finally how to "weed out" bad information.

Exercise I

Directions: Complete one or more of the following to integrate reading and using online texts.

1. Perform a search for the state of Hawaii. Suggested search engines are Google.com, Bing.com, Yahoo.com, and Ask .com. Search engines usually return ten or so websites per page. Using these results, review three to five of the returned choices. Look for one source that looks like an encyclopedia article on the topic.

2. Determine if the entry is user edited, or if it is from a valid source such as a commercial company like World Book.

3. Next, review a choice that is in the form of a blog or forum where users have commented on the published content.

4. Next, look for a visual source such as YouTube.

5. Finally, look for a web page that displays an entry that was published by a university or other "expert voice." This kind of web page may be a study that was conducted to prove or disprove a hypothesis, for example.

6. Compare what you have found by creating a T-chart. Do this by drawing a large *T* on a blank piece of paper and writing "State of Hawaii" on the top part of the *T*; then write similarities in the left column and differences in the right column. Include the URL (this is the http:// address).

Suggested Directions for Unit X

1. Have students complete one or more of the directions in Exercise I to integrate reading and using online texts.

2. Many of these activities require online access. Consider reserving the computer lab or allowing students to bring their own device if school policy permits. These assignments can also be assigned as homework. Internet access must be available in the student's home or the student may need access to the Internet elsewhere if it is not available at home.

3. It is recommended the teacher preview these assignments online to understand the expected search engine results for the suggested exercises. Remember, search engine results change frequently.

STUDENT TEXT

Exercise II

1. Find a classic book from the library, such as Jack London's *The Call of the Wild.* Read the first few pages of the first chapter.

2. Then, find the book online and read the same passage. Classic books are usually available in the public domain for free.

3. Write a reflection on which text was easier to read and why. What are the pros versus cons of reading printed text to its online equivalent?

_____

_____

_____

_____

_____

_____

4. Summarize your findings.

_____

_____

_____

_____

_____

_____

(continued)

Exercise III

1. Search for online reading speed and comprehension tests. Suggested search engines are Google.com, Bing.com, Yahoo.com, and Ask.com.

2. Follow the directions of the website to determine your level of reading speed online and the amount you comprehend.

3. Print out your results from the web page (if this option is available).

4. Continue to make reading online a priority so you will improve speed and accuracy.

5. Chart your progress throughout the school year by attempting to read more online offerings.

6. Present your findings at the end of the school year or term.

Exercise IV

1. Choose to read something for pleasure online for at least 30 minutes. Select something age-level/grade-level appropriate.

2. At the conclusion of the reading session, write a reflection of what you liked and what you disliked about reading for pleasure from a digital medium.

_____

_____

_____

_____

_____

3. Then, read something in traditional print for at least 30 minutes. At the conclusion of the reading session, write a reflection of what you liked and what you disliked about reading for pleasure from traditional print.

_____

_____

_____

_____

_____

4. It is suggested that you read similar types of material for this exercise.

(continued)

5. After completing reading both online and in traditional print format, rank your preference between reading online and reading from print. Indicate your reasons why in the space provided.

_____

_____

_____

_____

Exercise V

1. Choose a topic that interests you and read an online story or article for pleasure on that topic.

2. When you are on the web page, notice if there are any advertisements, videos, or other animations displayed on the screen. Make a list of those items you see on the screen (besides the text of the online story or article).

_____

_____

_____

_____

_____

3. Depending on what you listed, did you find any of these other "things" distracting while reading online?

_____

_____

_____

_____

_____

4. Did the online story or article page you were reading from contain any pictures or illustrations? Displays of images or illustrations leave little room for imagination, limiting our ability to form our own mental pictures to illustrate what we are reading. Make a list of what you see on your web page (not including the actual text you are reading).

_____

_____

_____

_____

_____

4. Review the steps in Exercise V with students. Demonstrate how to complete #1 prior to asking students to do the other steps.

Additional Suggestions

1. The activities in this unit are only a beginning toward the achievement of its goals. Reading and using online texts for learning or pleasure takes skill and practice. We encourage teachers to investigate ways to help students discover more about their own learning styles and to incorporate activities like the ones in this unit into the ongoing curriculum of your classroom. Some educators have made the shift from using traditional lessons where textbooks or supplemental texts are used (perhaps exclusively) to utilizing more online texts when possible or appropriate. This will allow students to become more confident in their online reading ability, speed, and comprehension. When research projects are involved, students are encouraged to utilize the search methods (follow the examples in the exercises) to properly know how to search and decipher reputable websites for research. Continue to monitor progress throughout any lessons where search engines are being utilized to ensure compliance. It is important to promote the importance of printed text in addition to online text.

STUDENT TEXT

Unit X Summary

- Reading and using online texts presents many different challenges for students.

- Proper tools and practice can provide a beneficial supplement to sources found in print media.

- The Internet contains a wealth of information—electronic books, research databases, journals, blogs, and other sources widely available free to users.

- Understanding that the Internet is a user-edited phenomenon will help you understand that you must be a discriminating consumer when it comes to text, articles, or facts you find online.

- Practicing using the Internet to read and decipher information will improve your speed and comprehension.

Suggested Retrieval Activities

As part of closure and retrieval of information learned, ask students to do one or more of the following:

- Have students practice reading online during class time (or on their own time) for pleasure for at least 30 minutes per session. This will help students continue to improve speed and comprehension, and work around distractions with online reading.

- As the class works through these units (and other classwork outside of *The hm Learning and Study Skills Program*), continue to use online reading sources (in lieu of print materials normally used to cover content). This will help students continue to improve speed and comprehension, and work around distractions with online reading.

- Consider downloading the electronic version of *The hm Learning and Study Skills Program* and using portions of this text in an electronic format with students.

STUDENT TEXT

Technology Adaptation

- Create an online account with your school or local library. Download content reading to your smart phone, tablet, computer, or other device. Mix your reading with text and online versions. Over a period of time, determine what reading you prefer by your speed, how much you comprehend, and if you are more likely to read using online or printed texts.

- Check with your local newspaper to see if online subscriptions are free or at a reduced rate to students or schools. Make it a goal to read at least three news stories per day. Choose one of a current national event, one of a current local event, and one article of your choosing. If online newspapers are not available, attempt to do this project using a website such as MSN, *USA Today*, or news from your local radio or television station.

- On your next school project, use the Internet to conduct research using the school or local library. Explore databases with the help of a librarian or teacher.

UNIT XI
USING A DICTIONARY

The dictionary is an essential tool for vocabulary acquisition. In today's society, dictionaries are available in print format, online, and in dedicated apps for tablet and mobile devices. Yet students often disregard this tool because they lack the skills for its effective use. Students often avoid acquiring these skills because they perceive a dictionary as difficult, tedious, and boring. Awareness of students' reticence may help to minimize their resistance to learning the uses of a dictionary.

Before having students work through this unit, it is suggested to examine the dictionary skills they already have. For this unit to be effective, students must possess at least some proficiency in the following skills:

1. Basic alphabetizing skills

2. Use of phonetic keys

3. Recognition of the abbreviations of parts of speech

4. Use of guide words

5. Recognition of what a dictionary entry is

6. Ability to choose a definition to match context

This exercise will require a class set of dictionaries or access to dictionary alternatives using an online source. If students need practice with these skills, consider focusing on different parts of dictionary usage over a period of several weeks. At the beginning of each class, have students work with one aspect of a dictionary for several minutes. For example, you might say:

"Find two meanings where the word *pick* is used as a noun."

"How many dictionary entries are there for the word *up*?"

It is important to correct these exercises immediately and discuss the sources of errors.

Such dictionary skill exercises are also helpful in the building of listening and direction-following skills. Other exercises are explained in the "Additional Suggestions" section for this unit.

Suggested Directions for Unit XI

Please note: Completing the challenge pre-exercise will require a class set of dictionaries or access to a dictionary or an alternative using an online source. The answers have not been provided because they will vary from source to source. Be sure students do the challenge pre-exercise at least a day before doing the rest of this unit.

Class Period I

1. Pass out dictionaries or provide directions for students to access dictionary alternatives using an online source. There are many available options in the Apple or Android app store. Another option is to consider using Google and have students type the following in the Google search bar: "Define: *word*" (where *word* is the term to be defined)—for example, "Define: dandelion." Another option is to use www.dictionary.com.

2. Students can work in pairs if necessary, but it is essential they all have the same dictionary or access to the same online dictionary or source.

3. Read over the challenge pre-exercise with students. Then give the following directions. Pause between directions to give students time to work.

   I am going to give you a set of directions. I will say the directions only once. You must listen and follow them.

   Find the spaces for word #1.

   Number 1: Spell the word *card* in the space provided.

   Number 2: Look up the word. Write the guide words for the word *card* on the line provided.

   Number 3: How many entries does the word *card* have? Write this number on the line provided.

   Number 4: Look at entry number #3. Write down what part of speech entry #3 is on the line provided.

   Number 5: Look at the sentence. Which entry and definition best fit the way *card* is used in this sentence? Write down your answers in the spaces provided.

   Find the spaces for word #2.

   Number 1: Spell the word *level* in the space provided.

   Number 2: Look up the word. Write the guide words for the word *level* on the line provided.

   Number 3: How many entries does the word *level* have? Write this number on the line provided.

   Number 4: Look at entry number #1. Write down what part of speech entry #1 is on the line provided.

   Number 5: Look at the sentence. Which entry and definition best fit the way *level* is used in this sentence? Write down your answers in the spaces provided.

Find the spaces for word #3.

Number 1: Spell the word *hush* in the space provided.

Number 2: Look up the word. Write the guide words for the word *hush* on the line provided.

Number 3: How many entries does the word *hush* have? Write this number on the line provided.

Number 4: Look at entry number #2. Write down what part of speech entry #2 is on the line provided.

STUDENT TEXT

Challenge! Pre-exercise Activity

The dictionary or an online dictionary is a valuable resource. When you were learning language skills, it was most likely an early reference book that you became familiar with. Since you are already familiar with a dictionary, the challenge will allow you to demonstrate how quickly you can locate and use information from the dictionary.

Word #1

1. _____

2. _____

3. _____

4. _____

5. After dinner tonight, do you want to play a game of cards?

   entry _____ definition _____

Word #2

1. _____

2. _____

3. _____

4. _____

5. Please put the advertisements at eye level so everyone who comes into the store can see them.

   entry _____ definition _____

(continued)

121

Word #3

1. _____

2. _____

3. _____

4. _____

The Dictionary: A Complicated Resource

If you had any trouble with the challenge pre-exercise activity, do not worry. This unit will help you to learn more about how to use a dictionary.

Exercise I

Directions: Read sentence 1. If what the sentence says is true for you, put a check in the space before the sentence. Do the same for sentences 2–4. Then answer number 5.

1. _____ I have trouble locating words that I don't know how to spell.

2. _____ I do not use guide words to help locate information.

3. _____ I have difficulty choosing the meaning that fits the context of the sentence.

4. _____ I have difficulty figuring out how a word is pronounced.

5. List any other problems you might have when using a dictionary.

_____

_____

_____

Introduction

You may have discovered that using a dictionary can be a frustrating experience. You want to learn about the meaning of a word, so you look it up in the dictionary or access the dictionary using an online dictionary source. But instead of finding one meaning, you find many different ones! What do you do then?

This unit will help you learn how a dictionary is organized and how you can make better use of it.

Day 2

1. At the beginning of the class, divide students into small groups of two to four members. Distribute a dictionary to each student or provide guidance on students accessing a dictionary using an online source or dictionary alternative.

2. Read the introduction aloud to students, or have students read it aloud. Discuss the first section of the directions for Exercise II, and ask students to answer this question. Go over the answer. If students reach different answers, briefly discuss how this happened.

STUDENT TEXT

Exercise II

Directions: Look up the word *run* in your dictionary or access a dictionary using an online source or dictionary alternative. Read through its many meanings. How many different meanings are listed for the word *run*? Write the number of different meanings in the space provided.

Answers may vary.

Read the following sentences carefully. Find the best definition for the word *run* as it is used in each sentence. Write the correct definition on the line under each sentence.

Example

"Run and call the vet," she ordered. "I can't seem to give her the help she needs with the calf."

1. "I can *run* faster than you," he snarled at me from the starting line.

   to go faster than a walk

2. She had a *run* in her tights.

   a ravel in a knitted fabric

3. The dog was not used to his collar and chain. He used to have the *run* of the whole neighborhood.

   freedom of movement

4. She decided to *run* for attorney general even though a woman had never held that office before.

   enter into an election

5. Even with the critics' praise, the play only had a three-month *run* on Broadway.

   an unbroken course of performances

(continued)

---

6. We wait eagerly for the salmon to *run* each year.

to go upriver to spawn

7. His fingers seemed to fly over the clarinet as he played the *runs* in the sonata with ease.

a rapid scale or passage

8. He always liked the Phoenix to Los Angeles *run* with its long stretches of open road.

a route traveled with regularity

9. The motorcycle was *run* off the road by a truck.

forced or pushed

10. The ship's captain wanted to *run* the blockade, but the admiral overruled his command.

slip through or break through

3. Read the second part of the directions for Exercise II aloud. Go over the example with the class. Then have your students work through this exercise either individually or in pairs. When they have completed the exercise, go over it orally.

STUDENT TEXT

Exercise III

Directions: Use a dictionary or access a dictionary using an online source or dictionary alternative. Write the best meaning for the way *trace* is used in each of the following sentences on the line below each sentence.

Example

There are *traces* of poison in the dead man's body.

small amount

1. He carefully *traced* the treasure map onto the see-through paper.

drawing by placing a transparent piece of paper over a map

2. We found no *traces* of the lost dog.

a sign that something has passed by

(continued)

124

3. She looked at the old homestead with a *trace* of regret in her eyes.

   hint or slight evidence

4. The *trace* from the stem to the leaf carries nitrogen that is needed for photosynthesis.

   one or more of the vascular bundles supplying a leaf or twig

5. We *traced* the bear tracks to the stream.

   to be guided by marks or signs

6. The lesson was designed to *trace* the rise and the fall of the Roman Empire.

   to review in outline form

7. She examined the graph that the machine had drawn by measuring his heartbeat. The *traces* showed possible signs of heart weakness.

   a mark or sign made by an instrument that records

8. The *traces* snapped, and the frightened horse ran off as the wagon rolled to a bumpy halt.

   either of two straps attached to an animal and to the vehicle that is drawn by the animal

9. She *traced* her ancestry back to the first Dutch settlers.

   to be guided by marks or signs

10. A tiny *trace* in the watch had broken, stopping the movement of the hour hand.

    connecting bar or rod

4. Exercise III can be used as further class work or as homework.

Additional Suggestions

1. Have students make up their own imaginary words. Then ask them to create dictionary entries for their imaginary words and use the words in sentences.

2. Have students make up imaginary words and write them phonetically, using a dictionary pronunciation key. They can exchange words with a partner and take turns pronouncing the imaginary words.

3. Explore homographs like these:

ob jecŧ   ób ject

reć ord   re corḋ

coń sole   con solé

Help students discover that such words not only have different pronunciations and different meanings but are also different parts of speech.

4. Have a dictionary word a day. Select words that have prefixes and the possibility of adding suffixes. Play with the word by adding the suffixes and discussing how suffix variations affect both meaning and part of speech. Offer the word in different contexts to show nuances in meaning. Consider having students make colorful illustrations showing how the same word can have many different applications.

5. Have students take on the responsibility for discovering a new daily word and sharing it with the class. Having this responsibility, students will refine their skills and share new information with the class. Students may use a printed dictionary or access a dictionary using an online source or dictionary alternative.

STUDENT TEXT

Unit XI Summary

One word can have many different meanings. You can use the dictionary to learn about the various meanings of a word and to figure out which meanings you need to learn. In today's society, dictionaries are available in print format, online, and in dedicated apps for tablet and mobile devices.

The dictionary can also give you other helpful information about a word:

1. how the word is pronounced;

2. the part or parts of speech of the word;

3. examples of how the word can be used;

4. various forms of the word: for example, plural, past tense, and so on; and

5. any special uses of the word.

Suggested Retrieval Activities

As part of closure and retrieval of information learned, ask students to do one or more of the following:

- Create a crossword puzzle with a free online program using vocabulary words from current daily lessons. Add additional words to the puzzle that will challenge students and allow them to use a dictionary for reference when solving the crossword.

- Give students an index card, and ask them to record the unit's instructional objectives. Tell them to explain whether or not the objective was met and to justify the answer.

STUDENT TEXT

Technology Adaptation

- Investigate the many types of dictionaries available to users today: printed format, online, and in dedicated apps for tablets and mobile devices. Find a new and useful dictionary and share findings with the class.

- Conduct an Internet search on the topic of advantages and disadvantages of using an online dictionary. Record and report the findings to classmates.

UNIT XII
IMPROVING YOUR VOCABULARY

Most educators and linguists believe that vocabulary acquisition is encouraged by a wide variety of reading. They also agree that learning the skills to use context clues significantly aids children in mastering new vocabulary.

Vocabulary lists can be useful. However, the evidence indicates that children can incorporate new words into their vocabulary most effectively if they have seen the words in use.

This unit focuses on two kinds of skills:

1. Developing the student's ability to recognize the context in which words appear in writing; and

2. Developing the student's ability to recognize context clues and use them for gaining an understanding of unknown or unfamiliar words.

When a child begins to recognize unknown words within their contexts, he or she becomes more aware of acquiring new vocabulary. When a child learns that he or she can often figure out the meanings of unfamiliar words from their contexts, he or she has acquired a powerful tool for increasing his or her vocabulary.

STUDENT TEXT

Introduction

Your vocabulary includes all of the words that you can understand and use in your thinking, speaking, writing, and reading.

Did you know that the average elementary school student increases his or her vocabulary by about 1,000 words every year? The average junior high or middle school student increases his or her vocabulary by almost 2,000 words each year!

One important way that you learn new words is through your reading. However, when you are reading, there are some problems that you may have in learning about unknown or unfamiliar words.

1. By now, you probably can read quickly enough so that you may skip over words without realizing that you don't understand them.

(continued)

---

2. To look up a word in the dictionary, you have to stop reading. This interrupts the flow of your reading.

3. When you use a dictionary, you must be able to choose the correct meaning from all the meanings listed.

This unit will help you to learn ways to solve these problems.

Suggested Directions for Unit XII

1. Divide the class into small groups of three or four students. Have the students take turns reading sections of the introduction aloud to the class, or read it aloud to them.

2. Then go over the directions to Exercise I. Read the three paragraphs aloud to students. Then ask students to write definitions for the italicized words. Consider having them do this individually or in groups.

STUDENT TEXT

Exercise I

Directions: Your teacher will read the two paragraphs that follow to you. Pay careful attention to the italicized words. Think about the meaning of these words. When your teacher has finished reading, write the definitions of the italicized words on the lines that follow.

Paragraph 1

I wish they hadn't been so worried about us. Jeannie and I had only taken the canoe for a quick trip down the lake. The day had been a breezy and blue one with lots of sunshine. The sunlight gleamed off the *ridges* of the waves. We tried at first to paddle, but the wind was so strong that it controlled our course. Since our paddling was useless, we *eased* ourselves down and rested against the cushions. We didn't know that sitting on the floor of the canoe was the best thing to do to keep the canoe *upright*.

Paragraph 2

As the wind grew stronger and the waves rose higher, the canoe began to rise and fall. We would be about to topple over the *crest* of a wave when our well-*dispersed* weight would balance us. Then we would slide easily down the watery slope. *Peering* over the boat's edge was like looking down from a roller coaster. We were rising and falling with each huge, rolling wave.

ridges _raised lines or strips that are higher than the rest of the substance_ _____

eased _moved slowly, gently_ _____

upright _erect, right side up_ _____

crest _top_ _____

(continued)

dispersed *spread around* _____

peering *looking* _____

Learning about New Words

When you come across an unknown or unfamiliar word in your reading, you can learn its meaning in two ways.

1. You can look up the word in the dictionary, glossary, or thesaurus.

2. You can often figure out the meaning of a new word by looking carefully at the meaning of the words and phrases around it. This is called getting the meaning from *context clues*. Some of you may have used this method in Exercise I.

    A *context* is the setting in which something is found. For example, a museum is a context in which paintings are displayed. A gym is a context in which people play basketball. You expect to find certain things because of the context.

    In language, *context* means the words and sentences around any particular word. *Context clues* are familiar words and phrases in a sentence or paragraph. These are words that you know. From these familiar words, you can often figure out the meaning of an unknown word.

    Example: Many animals are *extinct,* such as dinosaurs.

    extinct means *no longer in existence* _____

3. Before going over the definitions of the italicized words, have students turn to "Learning about New Words." Read this section aloud to students, and discuss it throughout the reading. Go over the example.

4. Turn back to Exercise I. Go over the definitions, and briefly discuss the context clues available for each italicized word in the passage.

STUDENT TEXT

Exercise II

Directions: Read the rest of the story about the canoeing adventure that follows. When you find a word that stops you because you are not sure of its meaning, underline the word.

I didn't worry. Jeannie and I were both strong swimmers. The shore wasn't very far away if the canoe decided to turn us into the foaming waters. I daydreamed that we were sailors on the ocean, conquerors of the deep. Poseidon, with all his power, could not entice us to his kingdom.

The ride finally stopped on the southwest side of the vast lake. The canoe came to a natural halt where the waters lapped gently against a small island. Suddenly we realized that we could never paddle back against those waves.

(continued)

We would have to wait. The lake would become still toward evening. Jeannie and I climbed out of the canoe and found a healthy patch of blueberries. While we devoured the blueberries, we felt completely carefree. Neither of us realized that we were in big trouble.

Then I spied my uncle. He came in a motorboat. The boat slapped against the waves and sprayed water high into the air. He had come looking for us, probably half expecting the canoe to be capsized with two victims floating facedown beside it. I knew he was relieved that we were alive. I also knew that his relief would soon turn to anger because we had been so foolish and had caused everyone at home to worry. I stood staring at my toes and felt the exhilaration of the day pour out of me.

5. Go over the directions for Exercise II and Exercise III with students. Then have them work through these exercises in their groups. When the groups have completed both exercises, go over the words they under-lined and the definitions they constructed. Focus the discussion on how they used context clues.

STUDENT TEXT

Exercise III

Directions: On the lines for the new words that follow, write the words that you have underlined in the canoeing story. Then try to figure out the meaning of each word that you have listed from its *context clues*. Write your meaning in the space to the right of the word.

New Words

Meaning

(continued)

Exercise IV

Directions: Choose the best meaning for the numbered words below from the canoeing story. Mark an *x* on the line in front of the best meaning. Look at the word *vast* below as an example.

Example

vast	a. ___ blue	c. ___ shallow	
	b. ___ far	d. _x_ huge	

1. devoured   a. ___ ate   c. ___ smashed

              b. ___ threw around   d. _x_ ate hungrily

2. spied   a. ___ looked at   c. _x_ spotted

        b. ___ looked secretly   d. ___ noticed

3. Poseidon   a. ___ a whale   c. _x_ god of the sea in Greek mythology

            b. ___ a king   d. ___ my uncle

4. capsized   a. ___ head size measure   c. _x_ turned over

          b. ___ thrown down   d. ___ collapsed

5. victim   a. _x_ someone who is hurt   c. ___ the target or injured

        b. ___ the weaker one   d. ___ feeling sad

6. relieved   a. ___ replacement   c. ___ jump around

          b. _x_ let go of worry   d. ___ feel a little better

7. exhilaration   a. ___ feeling of   c. ___ smashing disappointment

             b. ___ feeling of sadness   d. _x_ feeling of great excitement

8. conquerors   a. ___ sailors   c. ___ great boats

           b. _x_ ones who gain control   d. ___ captains

6. Have students do Exercise IV individually. Go over in class. If there is not time for this exercise, assign it for homework and go over it the next day.

7. Read aloud "How Can You Learn New Words from Your Reading?" or have students take turns reading sections aloud. Discuss briefly.

STUDENT TEXT

How Can You Learn New Words from Your Reading?

1. Keep a special section in your notebook for new words. In this section, write down all the new words that you come across and their meanings.

2. When you come across a word from your reading that you do not fully understand, first try to figure out its meaning from *context clues*.

3. When you cannot figure out the meaning of a new word from its *context clues*, you need to look it up in the dictionary to know what the word means.

Additional Suggestions

1. If students have difficulty working with context clues, let them work with the "cloze" procedure. The "cloze" procedure is a method of deleting specific words from a prose passage and then asking the student to supply the missing words.

   Example:

   When you have a cold, it is a good idea to stay home in _____. You should take two aspirin and _____ plenty of liquids.

   This kind of exercise gives students another way of learning about the uses of context clues.

   Using the "cloze" procedure, you can review vocabulary words that illustrate content taught in class. For example, if teaching conceptual words such as *democracy, communism, dictatorship,* and so on, photocopy a text, blank out the designated words, and have the students use context to fill in the blanks.

2. Design exercises using the reading from the current curriculum so students can practice decoding words from context. As students become adept at decoding words by using context, begin to teach them specific context clues. Examples of specific context clues are restating or defining, comparing or contrasting, making inferences, and creating a mood.

3. Use a context clue exercise that employs imaginary words, such as this one. Look at the imaginary words *snire* in the sentences below.

   The creature lowered his head, his eyes blazing. He aimed his snire at his enemy and breathed a flame that consumed her in seconds.

You know that a *snire* is *something* because the creature aimed *it*. But what kind of *thing* is it? Figure out all that you can about the word *snire* from its context.

When the students are finished, let them share their definitions with each other and discuss the variations. Students may work this kind of exercise in pairs or small groups.

4. Have students keep vocabulary notebooks. Tell them they have to enter three to five words each week. They must also enter the context and the definition. They can use outside reading, television, textbooks, or class discussions as sources for words. For this system to work, check these notebooks often and establish grading criteria.

5. "Play" the following activity for several minutes for a number of days.

Give each student a chart listing common prefixes, roots, and suffixes, such as the lists that follow. Invite students to create imaginary words that use these prefixes, roots, and suffixes. Once a student has created an imaginary word, have her or him create a written context for the word. Then have students read what they have written. Have other students guess the meanings of the imaginary words. Consider grouping students in pairs for this exercise.

PREFIXES—meanings	ROOTS—meanings	SUFFIXES
PRE—before	SCRIBE, SCRIPT—writing	ER
POST—after	GEN, GENER, GENIT—birth, class	OR
EXTRA—outside	SOLUT—loosen	NESS
IN—not	VIS, VID—see	ENT, ANT
CONTRA—against	TERRA—earth	MENT
CON—with	LATERAL—side	AL
AD—to	HERE—stick	TION
INTER—between	GREG—gather, group	OUS, IOUS
RE—again		
BI—two		
MULTI—many		

6. Read aloud passages with difficult words but with accessible content. Prepare the students to listen for certain words beforehand. Encourage them to use the context of what is read to decode the meaning of the words. This is also a good way to review the listening skills taught previously in this program.

STUDENT TEXT

Unit XII Summary

A context is the setting in which something is found. In language, *context* means the words and the sentences around any particular word.

Context clues are familiar words and phrases in a sentence or paragraph. From these familiar words, figure out the meaning of an unknown word.

When seeing a new word while reading, first try to figure out its meaning from its context clues. If this is not possible, look it up in the dictionary.

Suggested Retrieval Activities

As part of closure and retrieval of information learned, ask students to do the following:

- Write an advertising jingle that explains the importance of this.

- Write a 1–2 minute commercial to "sell" the lesson's content.

STUDENT TEXT

Technology Adaptation

- Use an Internet search engine to locate lists of prefixes, suffixes, and root words.

- Video your advertising jingle and put it on TeacherTube.

UNIT XIII
TAKING NOTES—MAPPING AND OUTLINING

This unit focuses students' attention on note taking as an important skill in itself. These skills for taking notes are best learned when they are reinforced through regular practice in the context of ongoing curriculum. Help students develop a note-taking system that works best for them. The measure of a student's note-taking capability is not the particular method employed but, rather, the usefulness of the notes to that student.

The unit suggests that (1) different individuals may use different methods in the same situation and that (2) any one student may want to use different note-taking methods in different situations. For example, a student who works well with linear, sequential processes may feel more comfortable and be more effective with outlining. A more visually oriented student, however, may flourish with the use of mapping. Also, even the most sequentially oriented student may find mapping valuable in a particular context, and vice versa.

This diversity indicates that for any particular note-taking situation, there may not be a "correct" set of notes. Instead, students may include a similar body of main ideas and important details but record them in very different ways. In giving students feedback about their note-taking skills, we suggest that the teacher primarily consider the effectiveness of their notes for them as individuals.

STUDENT TEXT

Introduction

In the unit about reading for meaning, it mentions *mapping* as a way of taking notes. This unit will help you to learn more about how to use *mapping*. It will also help you to learn about another way of taking notes called *outlining*.

Remember: Taking notes helps you to learn more about what you are reading or hearing. Also, when you take notes, you have a record to study when you have a test.

Why Take Notes?

"Taking notes is a lot of work. Why bother?"

Have you ever said this? Or heard a friend say it? Well, why should you take notes? Here are two good reasons for taking notes:

(continued)

---

1. When you take notes, you learn by writing the main idea and supporting details down on your paper. You will understand your reading better if you take a few minutes to write or type your notes. You will also remember the main idea and supporting details better. Typing your notes allows you to capture more information than writing notes by hand.

2. When you take notes, you have a record of what you read. You can use the record to study for tests.

Tips for Taking Notes

1. Your notes are for you! Take notes that make sense to you. This means that you can use words from your reading, too, but be sure you understand what your notes say.

2. When you take notes, you don't need to write in complete sentences. Write down only the words and phrases that tell you the main ideas and important details in your reading. You can also use abbreviations and symbols.

3. Don't write down everything in your reading. Write down only the main ideas and important details in your notes.

Suggested Directions for Unit XIII

1. Read the introduction aloud to the students. Then have a student read aloud "Tips for Taking Notes." Discuss each tip for clarity and emphasis.

STUDENT TEXT

Breaking Down Sentences

When you take notes, you want to write as few words as possible that tell the important ideas and information. One way to do this is *breaking down* the sentences in your reading into a few key words.

Look at the sentences that follow:

The Hunger Games is a 2008 science fiction novel by the American writer Suzanne Collins. It is written in the voice of 16-year-old Katniss Everdeen, who lives in the nation of Panem in North America.

Now look at an example of the notes from this sentence:

Hunger Games author—Suzanne Collins. Main character—Katniss Everdeen.

When you break down a sentence, try to write as few words as you can. But be sure to keep the important ideas and information.

Exercise I

Directions: Read the sentences that follow. *Break down* each into as few words as possible that tell the important ideas and information.

(*continued*)

1. The stories of Greek myths make good reading, for the gods and goddesses are dramatically filled with human emotion: love, hate, and jealousy.

   Greek myths—good reading—gods and goddesses filled with human emotion

2. Energy that was created from wind power could save the states of the windy north from their need to burn fuel.

   Northern states—wind energy can save fuels

3. The apple, the delicious fruit of the Garden of Eden, is an important fall harvest for the state of New York.

   Apple—important fall harvest in NY

4. In the late 1840s many people made a mad dash to California hoping to get rich through the discovery of gold.

   Late 1890s people went to CA seeking gold

5. The fair-haired, tall, and hard-fighting sailor of Scandinavia was known as the Viking.

   Viking—Scandinavian sailor and fighter

2. Have the students read "Breaking Down Sentences," or read it aloud to them. Discuss briefly. Have the students do Exercise I. Go over the exercise.

Note: Students may need more work in "Breaking Down Sentences." If this is the case, give them additional practice with other sentences.

STUDENT TEXT

Exercise II

Directions: Read the passage about Sioux Indian children. Complete the graphic organizer.

Sioux Indian children were taught to swim at a very early age. When the baby was two months old, its mother would take it to a quiet spot along the riverbank. She would place her hands gently under the baby's belly and place him or her into the shallow, warm water until it came up around him or her. Then suddenly the baby's sturdy legs would begin to kick and his or her arms to whip through the water. The next time the baby lasted a little longer, and by the third or fourth time the mother could take her hands away for a bit while the baby held his or her head up and dogpaddled for himself or herself.

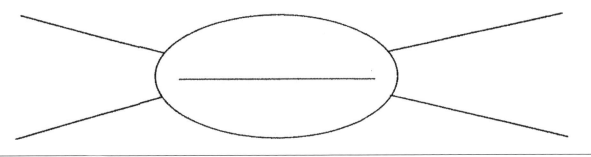

139

3. Have the students do Exercise II. Then go over the exercise. (Before the students begin, review the *reading for meaning* method with them.)

STUDENT TEXT

Another Way to Take Notes: Mapping with Numbers

You may have had some difficulty in drawing up your MAP for the paragraph about the Sioux baby. Maybe you asked yourself questions like these: How do I know which line I should start with? Can any detail go on any line? Or is there a place where each one belongs?

When the reading about which you are taking notes is organized in a certain order or sequence, you can still use a kind of *mapping* for your note taking. You do this by numbering the *supporting details* on your *map*. The details show the order of the sequence.

Look at the map that follows, and you will see an example of *mapping with numbers.*

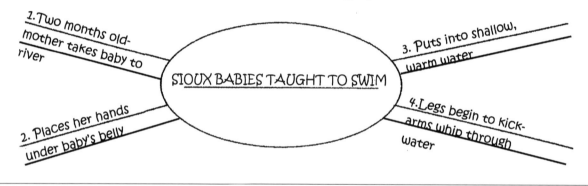

---

4. Read aloud "Another Way to Take Notes: Mapping with Numbers," or have students read it aloud. Look at the example together, and discuss for clarity and emphasis. Discuss when this way of taking notes might be useful. Then have students do Exercise III. Go over the exercise. Or do Exercise III on the board as a whole-class activity.

STUDENT TEXT

Exercise III

Directions: Try to map the paragraph that follows by *mapping with numbers.*

In its short lifetime, the butterfly goes through four complete changes. We can call these changes "Stages of Life for the Butterfly." The first stage is the egg stage. The adult female chooses a good food source to lay her eggs on. The second stage is the larvae or caterpillar stage. When the eggs hatch, the hungry caterpillars soon devour the leaves around them. They need to eat a lot because they don't eat at all in their third stage, and many don't eat in the fourth stage. Their third stage is spent resting in a cocoon or pupa chrysalis. Finally the adult emerges from the cocoon. In the last stage of life, the butterfly's main job is to mate and lay eggs.

(continued)

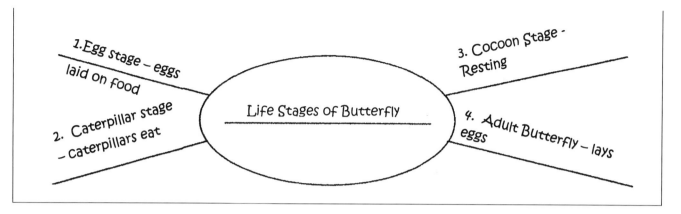

5. Read aloud "A Third Way to Take Notes: Outlining," or have students read it aloud. Discuss for clarity and emphasis. Discuss when this way of taking notes might be useful. Then have the students do Exercise IV. Go over the exercise.

STUDENT TEXT

A Third Way to Take Notes: Outlining

When a paragraph is organized into a certain sequence of events, it is easy to use a third way of taking notes called *outlining*. This is much the same as *mapping with numbers*, but the way the information is set up is different.

Following is a form for *outlining*.

Outline Form

I. Main Idea

   A. Supporting detail

   B. Supporting detail

   C. Supporting detail

How to Outline

1. Use a roman numeral to list main ideas.

2. Use capital letters to list supporting details. Indent each capital letter a little way to the right of the roman numeral.

(continued)

Exercise IV

Directions: Write your notes about the butterfly in the outline form.

    I. *Life Stages of the Butterfly* _____

        A. *Egg stage—eggs laid on food source* _____

        B. *Caterpillar stage—caterpillars eat* _____

        C. *Cocoon stage—resting* _____

        D. *Adult butterfly stage—lays eggs* _____

Exercise V

Directions: Read the paragraph that follows, and take notes for it on the outline form provided.

What causes hail? If you've ever had to run for cover to escape from the pounding of a hailstorm in the middle of what had been a hot and sticky day in July, you have probably asked yourself the same question. It usually hails in hot weather just before a violent thunderstorm. First cold air gets pushed up above the heavy, warm air. This causes strong upward winds. As it begins to rain, the raindrops are blown upward by these winds. The rain freezes in the cold upper air before it falls to the earth. Each time the droplets fall through the warm air, they gather more moisture. Each time the larger droplets are blown into the cold upper air, they freeze into larger ice balls. When this cycle repeats itself several times, you'll see hail that is the size of golf balls. So hail is created when the raindrops are blown into the colder air over and over again, causing them to freeze into hailstones.

    I. *Causes of Hail*

        A. *Hot air, thunderstorm* _____

        B. *Cold air over warm air—upward wind* _____

        C. *Rain blown up into cold air* _____

        D. *Rain freezes—hail* _____

        E. *Hail blown down, up many times before it hits the ground* _____

How Should *You* Take Notes?

You have tried three different ways of taking notes in this unit: mapping, mapping with numbers, and outlining. All three of these methods can be helpful to you.

Use a way of taking notes that makes sense to you. Experiment with these three ways of taking notes until you find the way that best fits the way that you learn.

You may want to use different note-taking methods at different times. Look carefully at the kind of reading that you're taking notes about. Then decide which way of taking notes will work best for you.

Remember: Your notes are for you! Take notes in your own words that make sense to you.

6. Have students do Exercise V. Go over the exercise. You may want to do this exercise as a whole-class activity.

7. Have students read "How Should *You* Take Notes?" Discuss for clarity and emphasis.

STUDENT TEXT

Cornell Note-Taking Guide

There are four easy steps in taking notes in this manner.

a. Draw a line vertically on the left side of a piece of paper.

b. Write important information from the lecture or text in the column on the right side of the paper.

c. After notes are completed, review the notes and write questions from the content in the margin on the left side of the paper.

d. Cover the right column, exposing only the questions on the left. Self-quiz or work with other students to learn the important concepts.

Use one of your textbooks and complete a Cornell note-taking guide. Use the form in the workbook, use another sheet of paper, or complete one electronically.

Cornell Notes

Questions	Notes
	Summary

Note: It is recommended that the Cornell Note-Taking Strategy, the Knowledge Chart Note-Taking Strategy, and the Text Structure Note-Taking Strategy be practiced by using the student's own text. These strategies work best with nonfiction text, so a student's science or social studies book would work well. For the sake of class discussion and teacher direction, all students should work from the same text while learning to use the strategy.

---

8. Another way to take notes is the Cornell note-taking strategy. The primary purpose of this note-taking method is to provide students with an organized and efficient method of taking notes from a lecture and/or text. This note-taking system also provides an easy-to-use study guide.

STUDENT TEXT

Knowledge Chart

There are six steps in completing this strategy.

a. Locate a text or visual images to share.

b. Using a piece of paper, divide it vertically into two columns of equal size.

c. At the top of the column on the left, write "Prior Knowledge." At the top of the column on the right, write "Need to Remember."

d. Prior to reading the assigned text, brainstorm what you already know about the topic and record the information in the column under "Prior Knowledge."

e. After reading the passage, list in the "Need to Remember" column notes from the text. Continue until you have listed several pieces of important information.

f. Using the information from both columns, work individually or in small groups to formulate questions for what you would still like to learn about the topic.

Use one of your textbooks and complete a knowledge chart. Use the form in the workbook or complete one electronically.

Knowledge Chart

Prior Knowledge	Need to Remember

---

9. The knowledge chart procedure is designed to help students think about what they already know and relate it to what is read from the text or heard in a lecture. This strategy supports understanding of the main idea as well as detailed information. Discuss the steps in the process with students.

STUDENT TEXT

Text Structure Strategy

To use the text structure strategy, follow the directions that follow.

a. Remember that authors use the structure of a text to facilitate understanding. If you do not understand the significance of these features or how to use them advantageously, you may have difficulty focusing, monitoring, and understanding written material.

b. Divide notebook paper into three equal vertical columns. Write "Text Structure" at the top of the column on the left, and write "Example" at the top of the middle column. Write "How It Helps" at the top of the column on the right side of the paper.

c. Complete the organizer by locating the specific support, giving an example of the support, and explaining how the support helps with comprehension. Sample supports include but are not limited to the following:

- chapter title

- headings

- subheadings

- photos

- bold print

- italics

- diagrams

- graphic organizers

- author questions

- key vocabulary

Use one of your textbooks and complete a text structure organizer. Use the form in the workbook, another sheet of paper, or complete one electronically.

(continued)

Text Structure

Text Structure	Example	How It Helps

10. The text structure strategy helps students understand how to use features within a text to facilitate under-standing and recall of information.

Additional Suggestions

1. Have students use their note-taking skills in as many different contexts as possible. For example, have students map or outline sections of a textbook. Help students build their note-taking skills gradually and thoroughly. Be careful to assign materials well within their reading levels while students are still learning mapping and outlining methods.

2. Collect and review the notes that students take. If at all possible, conference with the students indi-vidually about their progress.

3. Have students map or outline a process that they know well—for example, baking a cake, building a model, setting up a tent, or getting ready to come to school. This kind of exercise will also reinforce sequencing skills and the selection of main ideas.

4. Ask students to map or outline a descriptive paragraph. For example, have them map the traits of a main character or the main parts of a flower. By doing this sort of exercise, students will discover that the sequence of a map or outline can vary in many situations and still be valid.

5. After practice with short selections, go on to mapping or outlining more information such as a page of material, a chapter of a textbook (make sure to pick a text with distinct headings), or the plot of a well-known tale.

STUDENT TEXT

Unit XIII Summary

There are several good ways of taking notes: outlining, mapping, mapping with numbers, Cornell note taking, knowledge chart, and text structure.

Outlining

    I. Main Idea

        A. Supporting detail

        B. Supporting detail

        C. Supporting detail

        D. point also (supporting detail)

Mapping

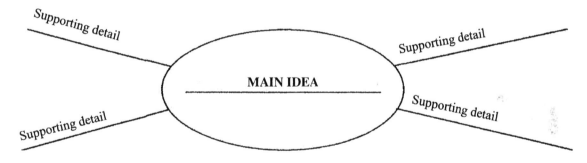

Mapping with Numbers

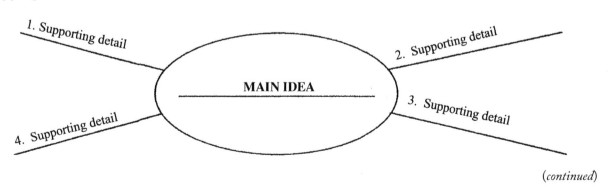

(continued)

Cornell Notes

Questions	Notes
	Summary

Knowledge Chart

Prior Knowledge	Need to Remember

Text Structure

Text Structure	Example	How It Helps

Suggested Retrieval Activities

As part of closure and retrieval of information learned, ask students to do one or more of the following:

- Ask students to choose the strategies that will be most beneficial in terms of learning. Have them explain to a classmate the reasons for the choices.

- Give each student an index card. Ask them to write a "postcard" to their parents explaining the day's lesson.

- Ask students to send an email to their parents explaining the day's lesson.

STUDENT TEXT

Technology Adaptation

- Use an Internet search engine to find other graphic organizers that can be used for taking notes.

- Use the open-source program FreeMind to make additional mind maps.

UNIT XIV
LISTENING AND TAKING NOTES

This unit provides an experience for students to integrate listening skills with note-taking skills.

For Exercises I and II in this unit, we have asked the teacher (1) to create and deliver a short talk and (2) to structure and lead a brief class discussion. We have not provided the content for these exercises because we are certain that what is teacher created for these purposes will be more engaging and useful to students than what we can provide for you. We suggest the teacher create content for these activities that is an integral part of ongoing curriculum.

Before beginning this unit, we also suggest reviewing additional suggestions 1–2. These suggestions are especially important for a group of students that has not had much experience with note taking. Students need to perceive the importance of developing a system of taking notes and of discussing these skills in class. They will make more sense of these skills if the skills are practiced within the existing curriculum. Additional suggestions 1 and 2 offer specific suggestions for the practice of these skills.

STUDENT TEXT

Introduction

Learning in school is accomplished in a number of ways. Listening carefully during a class discussion or while a teacher lectures can be enhanced by taking notes. While this program will teach you to take notes in a variety of forms, this unit will give you practice in listening and taking notes.

Listening and Taking Notes

Much of what you need to learn to do well in any class will be covered in the class itself. One way to learn more in class is to take notes.

Taking *brief* notes in class can help you learn in the following ways:

1. Taking notes in class can help you to find the main ideas of what is being said, because you will only want to write down the main ideas.

2. Writing down the main ideas as notes will help you to learn them better.

3. When you take notes in class, you can use your notes later to study for a test.

Suggested Directions for Unit XIV

1. Have students read the introduction and "Listening and Taking Notes." Discuss briefly.

STUDENT TEXT

How Do You Start?

Before you start to take notes from listening, decide which note-taking method best fits your way of learning. At first, use the method with which you are most comfortable, the one that seems the easiest for you.

Once you feel comfortable with one note-taking method, try using others. You may want to follow these suggestions:

1. You can use the *outline* method for any kind of organized talk. In an organized talk, the speaker has put the main ideas and important details into an order to share with you. Sometimes your teacher will put an *outline* on the board at the beginning of class or during class. Use this *outline* as a starting point for your *outline* notes.

2. You can also use the *mapping with numbers* method for an organized talk.

3. You can use the *mapping* method or the *mapping with numbers* method for taking notes during any activity that is less organized, such as a class discussion or question period.

4. The knowledge chart works well for class discussions. Just don't forget to brainstorm prior to the discussion what you already know about the topic.

5. The Cornell note-taking method works well for vocabulary words, taking notes from a text, or writing notes during a class discussion or lecture.

---

2. Read aloud "How Do You Start?" Discuss for clarity and emphasis. Have a student read the tips in "Tips for Taking Notes from Listening." Briefly discuss each tip.

STUDENT TEXT

Tips for Taking Notes from Listening

1. Be an *active* listener! Try to make sense of what the speaker is saying. Try to connect what the speaker is saying with what you already know.

2. If you can, "picture" in your mind what is being said.

3. Before you start to take notes, think about how the speaker has organized what he or she will say. For example, is there an outline on the board? Is it a class discussion? Then decide what method you want to use to take notes.

4. Try to spend most of your time listening. Figure out what the main ideas are, and write them down. Use only words and phrases, not complete sentences. *Remember:* your notes are for you; make sure they make sense to you!

5. When your teacher tells you that you will need to know something, be sure to write it down.

(continued)

Exercise I

Directions: Your teacher will give a talk for a few minutes. Take notes from the talk in the space below.

_____

_____

_____

_____

_____

_____

_____

_____

_____

_____

_____

_____

3. Have students read the directions for Exercise I. Put a brief outline for a five-minute talk on the board. Then ask students to decide what method they plan to use for taking notes from your talk. Deliver the talk to the class while students take notes.

STUDENT TEXT

Looking at Your Notes

Directions: Look carefully at your notes from Exercise I. Then answer the questions that follow.

1. What note-taking method did you use? _____

_____

2. How well did this method work for you? _____

_____

3. Do your notes make sense to you? _____

_____

4. How could you make your notes better or more helpful to you? _____

_____

4. Have students answer the questions in "Looking at Your Notes." (Discuss each of the questions with your students. Consider having several of your students put their notes on the board.)

STUDENT TEXT

Exercise II

Directions: Your teacher will lead a short class discussion. Take notes from the discussion in the space that follows.

_____

_____

_____

_____

_____

_____

_____

_____

_____

_____

_____

_____

_____

_____

---

5. Have students read the directions for Exercise II. Ask students to decide which note-taking method they plan to use. Then lead a five-minute class discussion. Remind students they will need to participate in the discussion and take notes about it.

STUDENT TEXT

Looking Again at Your Notes

Directions: Look carefully at your notes from Exercise II. Then answer the questions below.

1. Did you use the same note-taking method that you used for Exercise I?

   _____

   _____

(*continued*)

---

2. Explain why you chose the method that you used.

_____

_____

_____

_____

3. How is taking notes during a class discussion different from taking notes during a lecture?

_____

_____

_____

_____

4. Do your notes make sense to you?

_____

_____

_____

_____

5. How could you make your notes better or more helpful to you?

_____

_____

_____

_____

6. Ask students to evaluate their own notes by answering the questions in "Looking Again at Your Notes." Discuss their answers.

Additional Suggestions

1. Include practice in taking notes from listening as an integral part of the ongoing process of teaching note-taking skills. It is crucial to *both* provide repeated practice for students *and* give them feedback about the quality of their notes and, thus, the effectiveness of their note-taking skills.

2. Note taking involves an integration of many study skills. Many teachers see note taking as a reflection of what is learned daily in the classroom. These teachers also feel that note taking involves an integration of many classroom systems such as being prepared for class, being organized, and having accurate information for homework. For these teachers, taking notes in class is more of a *system* than a *study skill*. If this is the case, train students carefully. Think about the following:

a. Why do I want students to have notes?

b. Would it be a good idea to require a certain kind of notebook?

c. Do I want students to keep different kinds of notes? If the answer is "yes," help students set up specific sections of their notebooks.

d. How can I help my students retrieve information? It is most important that the students see the worth of keeping a notebook. Young note takers are impressed when they can store, find, and use information they have recorded.

e. How will I evaluate my students' notes? Before testing the students on information stored in their notes, help them evaluate the effectiveness of their notebook organization. Collecting notebooks and commenting on the strengths and weaknesses, quizzing students on the organizational structure, and pairing students so they can compare notes are some of the ways to evaluate the effectiveness of the note-taking system.

STUDENT TEXT

Unit XIV Summary

Much of what you need to learn for any class will be covered in the class itself. Taking *brief* notes in class can help you with this learning.

Use a note-taking method with which you are comfortable when you start. Later on, you may want to use different methods in different situations. For example:

1. You can use the *outline* method for any kind of organized talk. You can also use *mapping with numbers* for an organized talk.

2. You can use the *mapping* method or *mapping with numbers* for taking notes during a less organized activity, such as a class discussion.

Be an *active* listener! Try to make sense of what the speaker is saying. Spend most of your time listening. Figure out what the main ideas are, and write them down in words and phrases.

Remember: Your notes are for you. Take notes that make sense to you.

Suggested Retrieval Activities

As part of closure and retrieval of information learned, ask students to do one or more of the following:

- Ask students to write answers to the following:

  o What did we learn today?

  o So what? Why is it important?

  o Now what? How will I use this information to become a better student?

STUDENT TEXT

Technology Adaptation

- Choose a partner and pick a note-taking strategy to practice. Listen to an audio book or a podcast and take notes. Compare the notes with your partner.

UNIT XV
PUTTING A BOOK TOGETHER/TEXT FEATURES

This unit is designed to help students gain an understanding of the various parts of a textbook. Most students in the middle school years do not view their texts as sources or references. While they may have some awareness of the various parts of a text, like the glossary or the index, they tend not to use these sections of their books in an effective way.

This will involve students in creating examples of the various parts of a text other than the body of the book. These activities can help students to understand the structure of a textbook and to begin to view their texts as tools they can use for their own learning.

If students are not at all familiar with the parts of a textbook addressed in this unit (title page, copyright page, table of contents, body or text, glossary, index, bibliography), introduce them in a gradual way and employ the descriptions of these parts included in this unit as a review. For example, spend a few minutes at the beginning of class over a week or two teaching students about these parts of a textbook.

Suggested Directions for Unit XV

This unit should be worked as a whole-class project, and it will require approximately two periods of class time.

Students will be engaged in creating, sharing, and using parts of a "textbook." When examining this unit, consider how to have students share the parts of the "textbook" that they create. Keep in mind that what students create on the first day will be shared and used on the second day.

Use one of the following methods:

a. Have students write on large pieces of paper that can be hung up in the front of the room.

b. Have students write on the board if the classroom has sufficient board space.

c. Have students create the textbook electronically.

d. Have students record answers in the workbook.

STUDENT TEXT

Introduction

Almost every textbook has many different parts other than just the *body* or *text* of the book, that is, the written sections in each chapter. Most of your textbooks have all of the parts listed below:

- title page and copyright page

- table of contents

- body or text

- glossary

- index

- bibliography

When you know how to find and use all of these parts, your textbook can become more helpful to you in your learning.

In this unit, you will learn about the different parts of a textbook by putting a book together. The *body* of the "book" you will put together is actually an article called "Monkey Business."

Exercise I

Directions: *Survey* the article "Monkey Business."

Title Page and Copyright Page

The *title page* is the very beginning of a book. The *title page* tells you the title of the book. It also lists the author and publisher and where the book was published.

The *copyright page* is usually right after the title page. This page tells you who has the right to print the book and when the book was first printed.

Day I

1. Read the introduction aloud to students. Discuss briefly. Then have students do Exercise I; give them three minutes to conduct their surveys.

2. Have a student or students read "Title Page and Copyright Page" aloud. Then do Exercise II as a class. Do parts A and B orally; write part C.

STUDENT TEXT

Exercise II

Directions:

A. Find the *title page* in this study skills program, and locate the following information:

- What is the title of this book? Who is the author? Who published the book? Where was the book published?

B. Find the *copyright page* of this book. Locate the following information:

- Who has the right to print this book? When was this book first printed?

C. Using the title page and copyright page in this book as a source of information and as a model, make up a *title page* for "Monkey Business."

Table of Contents

The *table of contents* tells you what you will find inside the book. It lets you know about the main ideas that are covered in the book. The *table of contents* also tells you how many chapters there are in the book and on what page each chapter begins.

You can find the *table of contents* in the front of the book, usually right after the copyright page.

Exercise III

Directions:

A. Find the *table of contents* in this study skills program, and examine it.

B. Read over the article "Monkey Business." Decide what the chapter headings should be, and make a list of these headings.

C. Create a *table of contents* for "Monkey Business." Your table of contents should contain chapter titles and pages on which the chapters begin.

Table of Contents

1. *Introduction: A Brief History—page #113*

2. *Two Classifications—page #114*

3. *Old World Monkeys—page #114*

4. *New World Monkeys—page #115*

5. *Proboscis Monkey—page #115*

6. *Spider Monkey—page #116*

7. *Monkeys in Captivity—page #118*

3. If students could benefit from a review of the table of contents, the glossary, the index, and the bibliography, read aloud the descriptive sections about these textbook parts, or have students read them aloud. Discuss briefly. (This step can be omitted if students already have sufficient awareness of these textbook parts.)

4. Divide the class into work groups as follows:

   a. Have about 20 percent of students do Exercise III *and* Exercise VI.

   b. Have about 40 percent of students do Exercise IV.

   c. Have about 40 percent of students do Exercise V.

   If direction #3 was omitted, tell students to read the descriptions above their assigned exercises carefully before they begin work.

   Have students work on the assigned exercises. Tell them to follow the directions carefully. Also, give them the necessary materials for creating their group products, that is, newsprint and magic markers, or chalk/dry-erase markers and board space, or photocopies. Provide them with whatever instruction they need to make a product that can be easily shared.

5. Collect the finished group products at the end of the period.

STUDENT TEXT

Glossary

The *glossary* of a textbook is a lot like a dictionary for that book. It lists words that are new or unfamiliar to most readers and tells you how the words are pronounced, what part of speech they are, and what their meanings are.

The *glossary* covers meanings that are used within that book. It often does not list every meaning of a word as a dictionary would.

You can usually find the *glossary* at the end of the body of the book.

Exercise IV

Directions:

   A. Read the article "Monkey Business."

   B. There are 17 underlined words or terms in the body of "Monkey Business." Find all of these words or terms; make a list of them, and put the list into alphabetical order.

      PLEASE NOTE! A term is a group of words that have a particular meaning together. Some of the terms in "Monkey Business" are *animal behaviorists, endangered species,* and *hurdy-gurdy man.*

(continued)

162

In a *glossary,* terms like these are listed as if they were a single word.

_____

_____

_____

_____

C. Using context clues or a dictionary, write a glossary definition for each underlined word or term in the body of the article. Be sure to use the same meaning that is used in "Monkey Business."

_____

_____

_____

_____

_____

_____

_____

_____

_____

_____

_____

_____

_____

_____

_____

D. Put your words and definitions together so you have a *glossary* for "Monkey Business."

Glossary

animal behaviorist: a scientist who studies animal behavior _____

breed: to produce offspring or young _____

bushbaby: one kind of "pre-monkey," has large eyes that cannot move in their sockets _____

classification: category _____

continent: one of the grand divisions of land on the earth, of which there are seven: Asia, Africa, Europe, North America, South America, Australia, Antarctica _____

(continued)

163

decline: getting smaller, moving towards extinction

endangered species: a kind of animal whose population has become so small that it is in   danger of being wiped out

haunches: hips or hindquarters

hurdy-gurdy man: traveling musician who plays an accordian and has a monkey who begs coins for him

instinct: a kind of behavior in which an animal acts automatically; instincts are not learned but are part of the animal from birth

mammals: a class of animals that have backbones and nourish their young with milk

prehensile: adapted for seizing or grasping

primates: an order of mammals consisting of humans, apes, monkeys, and "premonkeys"

proboscis: a long, flexible snout or nose

tarsier: one kind of "pre-monkey," has large eyes that cannot move in their sockets

territory: an area of land that an animal lives in and will defend against intruders

tree shrew: the first "pre-monkey"

Index

An *index* lists specific names and ideas found within a book. This list is in alphabetical order. Numbers of the pages where ideas and names can be found are listed after the names and ideas.

Bushbaby, p. #114

Colobus monkey, p. #119

Endangered species, p. #116

Guenons, p. #119

Howler monkey, p. #119

Hurdy-gurdy man, p. #116

Langur, p. #119

Macaque, p. #119

Mangabeys, p. #119

Marmoset, p. #119

Monkeys as pets, p. #118

New World monkeys, p. #114

Old World Monkeys, p. #114

Premonkey, p. #114

Probiscis monkey, p. #115

Spider monkey, p. #116

Tarsier, p. #114

Tree shrew, p. #114

Uakari, p. #119

Woolly monkey, p. #119

Zoos, p. #118

(continued)

You can usually find the *index* at the very back of the book. Some reference books have a separate volume for the index.

Exercise V

Directions:

A. All of the words and terms in the list that follows appear in the article "Monkey Business." Put this list of words and terms into alphabetical order.

Bushbaby	*New World monkeys*
Colobus monkey	*Old World monkeys*
Endangered species	*Owl monkey*
Guenons	*Pre-monkey*
Howler monkey	*Proboscis monkey*
Hurdy-gurdy man	*Spider monkey*
Langur	*Tarsier*
Macaque	*Tree shrew*
Mangabeys	*Uakari*
Marmoset	*Woolly monkey*
Monkeys as pets	*Zoos*

B. Read the article "Monkey Business." As you read, locate the words from the previous list in the body of the article. Each time that you find a word in the body of the article, write that page number after the word in the list.

Make sure you find each time that each word appears.

C. Put all of the words and page numbers together, so you have an index for "Monkey Business."

Bibliography

A *bibliography* is a list of references that an author has used to help him or her write a book or article. References can include books or articles. A *bibliography* lists the references alphabetically by the author's last name.

(continued)

A *bibliography* is set up in the following way: Author's last name, First name. *Title.* Place published: Name of publisher, Date published.

You can usually find the *bibliography* just before the index at the back of the book.

Exercise VI

Directions:

A. Arrange the references for "Monkey Business" listed in correct alphabetical order.

B. Write a *bibliography* for "Monkey Business." Be sure to punctuate everything correctly.

Whitlock, Ralph, *Chimpanzees.* Milwaukee: Raintree Children's Books, 1977. Morris, Dean. *Monkeys and Apes.* Milwaukee: Raintree Children's Books, 1977. Shuttlesworth, Dorothy. *Monkeys, Great Apes, and Small Apes.* Garden City, NY: Doubleday and Company, Inc., 1972. Leen, Nina. *Monkeys.* New York: Holt, Rinehart, and Winston, 1976. Annixter, Jane, and Paul Annixter. *Monkeys and Apes.* New York: Franklin Watts, 1976.

Annixter, Jane, and Paul Annixter. *Monkeys and Apes.* New York: Franklin Watts, 1976. _____

Leen, Nina. *Monkeys.* New York: Holt, Rinehart, and Winston, 1976. _____

Morris, Dean. *Monkeys and Apes.* Milwaukee: Raintree Children's Books, 1977. _____

Shuttlesworth, Dorothy. *Monkeys, Great Apes, and Small Apes.* Garden City, NY: Doubleday and Company, Inc., 1972. _____

Whitlock, Ralph. *Chimpanzees.* Milwaukee: Raintree Children's Books, 1977. _____

Monkey Business

Introduction: A Brief History

At zoos, people often find themselves standing in front of monkey cages. They stare at the intelligent animals that seem curiously like humans. Monkeys can use simple tools, and their hands twist and turn cleverly. Monkeys even seem to have emotions. Actually, monkeys are like humans in another way. They both belong to the same group

(*continued*)

tree shrew

bushbaby

of *mammals*, as do chimpanzees and apes. This group is called *primates*. All primates have grasping hands or feet, well-developed vision, and relatively large brains.

The primate story began many millions of years ago. A "pre-monkey" known as the *tree shrew* made its appearance on the earth about 70 million years ago. It preferred the high treetops where it could look down safely on the giants we know as dinosaurs. It was one of the first mammals. Since it was so tiny, the tree shrew was timid. It preferred hiding to fighting. Its clever, long fingers, a brain that was large for its size, and its ability in climbing made the tree shrew a survivor. It still lives today, long after the dinosaurs, on the island of Madagascar (a large island off the eastern coast of Africa).

The tree shrew, the *bushbaby*, and the *tarsier* are some of the animals we call "pre-monkeys." They are like monkeys in many ways, but they aren't as highly developed as monkeys are.

Notice the huge, staring eyes. Unlike "real" monkey's eyes, these eyes cannot move within their sockets.

tarsier

(continued)

167

The first of the "real" monkeys emerged about 30 million years ago. Unlike the "pre-monkey," monkeys have eyes that move in their sockets, arms and legs more useful for speedy climbing and running, hands better developed for holding, and a larger and more complicated brain.

Two Classifications

Monkeys come in all sizes, shapes, and colors. But they fit into two large _classifications_ or categories. These classifications are Old World monkeys and New World monkeys. They are put into these classifications because of where they are found. Old World monkeys are found in the rain forests of Africa and Asia. They are also found in the islands off these _continents_. New World monkeys are found in the rain forests of South America and Central America. A few can even be found in Mexico. There are many noticeable differences between these two kinds of monkeys.

Old World Monkeys

Old World monkeys are generally considered to have more intelligence than New World monkeys. They will often use simple tools, such as a stick for digging out delicious ants or a rock for killing small game. Their noses are more like human noses than those of New World monkeys are. They are narrow and point downward.

Old World monkeys have 32 teeth, the same as humans have. They have tough protective pads under their _haunches_.

At one time, _animal behaviorists_, scientists who study animal behavior, thought that Old World monkeys were more disagreeable than New World monkeys; Old World monkeys were believed to be more dangerous as they fiercely guarded their _territories_. Modern animal behaviorists disagree. They point to the poor conditions under which the first studies were made. The monkeys were kept in small cages, were not fed proper foods, and often were teased. No wonder the monkeys appeared to be fierce!

New World Monkeys

New World monkeys often have a long and agile tail; most Old World monkeys do not. This tail can be used as another hand for grasping and swinging. These tails are called _prehensile_ because of their grasping qualities.

The New World monkeys have broad and round noses. They rely on _instinct_ for survival. They rarely use tools as Old World monkeys do. Their bodies are generally longer and slimmer. This makes climbing and traveling through the trees easier. Almost all New World monkeys live in trees. Some Old World monkeys get too heavy to feel comfortable staying high up in the air on slender branches.

Proboscis Monkey

Proboscis means long-nosed in Latin. The bright-red head and the long nose of the adult proboscis make it one of the strangest-looking creatures in the animal world. The adult male's nose can reach three inches below its chin. Scientists believe this nose could be the sounding board for the long drawn out "honk" or "keehonk" of the proboscis. The proboscis lives in the rain forests of Borneo, an island in the western Pacific Ocean, and travels through the trees in large, noisy troops.

The proboscis is an example of an Old World monkey. It may weigh less than a pound at birth, but when full grown, the male can weigh up to fifty pounds. The female weighs about twenty-five pounds. The proboscis does not have sunken eyes like many monkeys. Its eyes are small, and it seems to look out intelligently. A baby proboscis's nose will start out looking much like any other monkey's nose. As the monkey matures, the nose grows, and the lips draw into a smile. It's almost as if the proboscis knows what a strange-looking character it is!

(continued)

Proboscis monkey watching from his treetop.

The proboscis eats large amounts of leaves. It also enjoys shoots from mangoes and other fruit. However, it is not an overworked monkey, constantly on the lookout for food. It eats when it wants to. It usually prefers to spend its time lounging on its back or sitting motionless among the tree leaves. The proboscis also enjoys an occasional swim in a tropical river or lake.

(*continued*)

Hunters value the proboscis monkey for its rust-colored fur. This is one reason why the proboscis is on the _endangered species_ list.

Proboscis male—his nose can be three inches longer than his chin!

Spider Monkey

One of the most common New World monkeys is the spider monkey. This monkey gets its name because of its "spider-like" appearance as it moves through the trees at remarkable speeds. Its prehensile or grasping tail helps it to be quick and agile. It uses its tail to climb high into the rain forests of South and Central America and Mexico. The tail can also help the spider monkey grab bits of food as it stretches down from the trees. The end of the tail has a patch of bare skin that is very sensitive. It can pick up a small fruit or a peanut.

Spider monkey reaching for delicate bits.

(_continued_)

The spider monkey usually travels in small bands or groups. However, up to thirty spider monkeys have been seen traveling together. Their voices cut through the rain forest in a high-pitched warning yelp. This sounds a lot like many barking terriers.

One of the spider monkey's favorite sports is wrestling. It does not like to swim, even though experiments have shown that it can swim quite well. The spider monkey prefers to hook its long tail on a branch and swing back and forth like a hammock.

The spider monkey is the monkey we picture traveling with the _hurdy-gurdy man_. The traveling musician would play his wind-up organ on the street as his spider monkey begged for coins.

Monkeys in Captivity

Monkeys do not usually adapt very well as pets. They seem quite happy and sweet when they are young but often grow up to be moody and unpredictable. They bite and spit at times and do cute tricks at other times.

Zoos keep many types of monkeys. These monkeys adapt very well if they have large, clean cages, which also have equipment for climbing and swinging.

"Hurdy-gurdy" man and his trained monkey.

(*continued*)

Besides having monkeys for people to watch, zoos want to help any monkeys that are an endangered species. Monkeys are hunted for food, fur, pets, and medical research. Also, each year more and more acres of rain forest are being cut down by farmers and builders. Monkey populations all over the world are on the _decline_. Since monkeys _breed_, or reproduce their young, very well in captivity, a well-kept zoo is an important place for them.

Some information about the kinds of monkeys you might find in a zoo is listed below.

Type of Monkey	Zoo Life Span	Home Continent
Colobus monkey	8–12 years	Africa
Guenons	20–30 years	Africa
Howler monkey	10–15 years	Central, South America
Langur	10–20 years	Asia
Macaque	25–30 years	Asia
Mangabeys	15–20 years	Africa
Marmoset	2–8 years	South America
Owl monkey	10–13 years	Central, South America
Proboscis monkey	4–10 years	Asia
Spider monkey	17–20 years	South, Central America
Uakari	5–9 years	South America
Woolly monkey	10–12 years	South America

If you go to a zoo, stand in front of the monkey cage and try to imagine being in the rain forests of South America, Central America, Africa, or Asia. Do not be surprised if you think you see a monkey look right at you and then seem to be laughing. The monkey may just think humans are strange-looking creatures!

Exercise VII

Directions: Answer the questions below, using the table of contents, the glossary, the index, and the bibliography that you have put together for "Monkey Business."

1. By looking at the table of contents, can you tell if this book will inform you about what monkeys eat? How do you know?

   No, there is no mention of what the monkeys eat.

(_continued_)

2. Use the glossary to help you answer this question: Can you give an example of an *instinct*?

   Answers may vary

3. Use the index to help you answer this question: What is unusual about the "pre-monkey's" eyes?

   The "pre-monkey's" eyes do not move in their sockets.

4. Use the bibliography to help you answer this question: Which book is the most recent source of information for "Monkey Business"?

   "Chimpanzees" and "Monkeys and Apes" were both published in 1977.

Day 2

1. Display or hand out the various parts of a "textbook" that students have created. Have students do Exercise VII individually. Go over the exercise.

STUDENT TEXT

Exercise VIII

Directions: Answer the questions below, using the parts of the article "Monkey Business" that you have put together. Then, in the marked space, write which part(s) of the book you used to help you answer the question.

Example

What chapter would you read if you wanted to learn about how monkeys live in zoos?

chapter 7

Part of the book: *table of contents*

1. Are you a mammal? Name three kinds of mammals.

   Yes; answers will vary.

   Part of the book: *glossary*

2. Where does the spider monkey live?

   South America, Central America

   Part of the book: *index and body*

(continued)

---

3. Where are Raintree Children's Books published?

   Milwaukee

   Part of the book: _bibliography_

4. What kind of question might you ask an animal behaviorist about your pet dog?

   Answers will vary.

   Part of the book: _glossary_

5. Are monkeys good pets? Why or why not?

   _No._

   Part of the book: _index and body_

6. Where would you find a description of the Proboscis monkey?

   Page #

   Part of the book: _index and body_

2. Read the directions for Exercise VIII aloud. Go over the example orally. Then have students do the exercise. Go over the exercise; discuss for emphasis.

Additional Suggestions

1. Have students create "book parts" for pieces of their own writing. Select a "book part" that would be a constructive addition to what they have written.

2. Develop worksheets that ask students to use the various parts of a textbook in involving and challenging ways.

STUDENT TEXT

Unit XV Summary

You can use your textbooks better to help you learn when you understand how the parts of a book fit together. Also, when you want to find out specific information, knowing the parts of a textbook and how to use them can save you time and effort.

(continued)

The main parts of a textbook are these:

1. The *title page* tells you the title of the book. It also tells you the author, the publisher, and where the book was published.

2. The *copyright page* tells you who owns the right to print the book and when the book was first printed.

3. The *table of contents* informs you what the chapters are in the book and on what page each one starts. It can also help you to find out what main ideas are covered within the book.

4. The *body* or *text* of the book includes all of the written sections in each chapter.

5. The *glossary* is like a dictionary for new or unfamiliar words used in the book. Words in a glossary are listed in alphabetical order; each listing tells you the meaning of that word as it is used in the book.

6. The *index* is an alphabetical listing of specific names and ideas found within a book. Numbers of the pages where the names and ideas can be found are listed after the names and ideas.

7. The *bibliography* lists all of the references, the books and articles that the author has used in writing the book.

Suggested Retrieval Activities

As part of closure and retrieval of information learned, ask students to do one or more of the following:

- Select a current textbook used at school. Locate the title page, table of contents, glossary, index, and bibliography. Explain the significance of each.

- Design a "commercial" that would encourage classmates to use the text features.

STUDENT TEXT

Technology Adaptation

- Note the features of an online text/article. How is the format of an online text different from a traditional text?

- Use a search engine to look for different online resources for making bibliographies and citations.

UNIT XVI
STUDYING AND TEST TAKING

This unit engages students in examining their own study environment and behavior. It also introduces students to a series of skills for answering the most common kinds of objective test questions.

"Testwiseness" involves understanding the various kinds of questions asked, the kinds of answers they require, and what thinking processes one can use to answer questions most effectively. The second part of this unit is based on the assumption that a student who is "testwise" will be able to show what he or she has learned more effectively. It seems only fair to help students understand how tests work so that they can accurately convey what they know to others.

STUDENT TEXT

Introduction: Studying—Finding the Right Environment

Studying means learning. When you are studying to be a musician, a carpenter, or a soccer player, you need the right *environment* for your learning. The *environment* is everything that surrounds you. For example, when you are learning to play a musical instrument, you need a quiet place where you can hear what you are playing and where no one will bother you.

When you are studying for school, you also need the right *study environment*. The first part of this unit will help you to think about what kind of *study environment* is good for you and the way you learn. It will also give you a few suggestions for how you might make better use of your study time.

Exercise I

Directions: Read the paragraphs, and follow the instructions listed.

Suzanne's teacher spent the first few days of school talking about the conditions in a good study or learning environment. He said that people have different learning styles and so different people learn best in different kinds of *study environments*. He wanted all of his students to experiment with different *study environments* and find out what helped them to learn better.

Suzanne tried many different conditions before she found the environment that was best for her. Her two most different experiments are in pictures that follow.

(continued)

Look at the pictures of Suzanne's two study environments. Then, on the lines that follow, write down all the differences you see.

Environment #1

Environment #2

Environment #1   **Environment #2**

_____   _____
_____   _____
_____   _____
_____   _____
_____   _____
_____   _____
_____   _____
_____   _____
_____   _____

Suggested Directions for Unit XVI

1. Read the introduction aloud, or have students read it to themselves. Discuss briefly.

STUDENT TEXT

Exercise II

Directions: Look at both of the lists you have made. Circle all of the conditions in both lists that would distract or bother *you* if you were trying to learn.

Now make a list on the lines that follow of what you would want in an environment that would help you study.

_____

_____

_____

_____

Tips for Studying

1. Each person seems to have good times of the day for learning. When do you learn best? In the morning, the afternoon, or the evening? Try to figure out when is the best time for you to study.

2. When you study at home, ask your family to help you by keeping things fairly quiet.

3. Get a small notebook to write down what you have to do for homework. Before you leave school, check your notebook. Then ask yourself, "What will I need to take home tonight?" Make sure you take everything you need home with you.

4. Have your materials together when you start to study. Ask yourself, "Do I need a pencil and paper? A dictionary? Anything else?"

5. How long can you pay attention when you are doing your schoolwork? Experiment to find out. If you can concentrate for fifteen or twenty minutes, plan to study for that long. Then do something active and fun for a few minutes before you start studying again.

6. Each time that you plan to study, set goals for yourself. These goals should be things that you can really do in the time you have. For example, you may not be able to read an entire book for a book report. Instead, decide how many chapters you can read, and try to reach your goal.

---

2. Have students do Exercise II. When they have finished, discuss their ideas for a good study environment. Have several students write their lists on the board, and discuss. Or have students discuss their lists in small groups. Find out which characteristics of a good study environment are most generally accepted by students, and list these on the board. Perhaps a few students could design a poster about study environment using the ideas that the class has generated.

3. Have students read "Tips For Studying" aloud. Briefly discuss each one.

STUDENT TEXT

How Do You Learn?

Some people learn best when they *hear* information. Others learn best by *writing* important details. Sometimes *picturing the facts* is a good way to learn. Another way to learn is to *try to connect* or make sense of how facts fit together. Most of us learn by combining these ways.

When you pay attention to how you learn best, you will be able to learn more effectively.

Exercise III: Part A

Directions: You will experiment to see how you learn the best. Look at the chart called "Facts about the First Five American Presidents." You will have five minutes to try to memorize the facts. Then you will be asked to fill in the blanks on a similar chart.

Think about ways that you learn the best. Try some of the following ways:

1. Say the facts aloud to yourself.

2. Study the lists. Then cover the lists and see if you can remember the information.

3. Write the facts on another piece of paper.

4. Think of the facts in a way that makes sense to you. For example: Of the first five American presidents, three of them were Democratic-Republican. Each of the first five presidents, except for John Adams, had eight years in office. James Monroe was famous for the Monroe Doctrine.

---

4. Read "How Do You Learn?" aloud. Discuss briefly.

5. Read the directions for Exercise III: Part A aloud, or have a student read them to the class. Discuss the directions and the techniques. Stress that students should experiment with techniques rather than take an actual test. Then have students do the exercise.

STUDENT TEXT

Facts about the First Five American Presidents

NAME	WHEN ELECTED	PARTY	FAMOUS FOR
George Washington	1789	None	First president General in the Revolution
John Adams	1797	Federalist	Helped write the Declaration of Independence First president to live in Washington

(continued)

NAME	WHEN ELECTED	PARTY	FAMOUS FOR
Thomas Jefferson	1801	Democratic-Republican	Author of Declaration of Independence Scientist farmer Architect
James Madison	1809	Democratic-Republican	Founder of Constitution Husband of Dolly Wrote 9 amendments
James Monroe	1817	Democratic-Republican	Hero of the Revolution Monroe Doctrine

Exercise III: Part B

Directions: See how many facts you remember. Fill in the blank spaces that follow. When you have finished, turn back to the previous chart and check your answers.

Remember: This is an experiment to see how you learn; this is not a test. It is more important to recognize how you learn than to pay attention to how many facts you remember.

Facts about the First Five American Presidents

NAME	WHEN ELECTED	PARTY	FAMOUS FOR
1. *George Washington*	1789	None	First president 2. *General in the Revolution*
John Adams	3. *1797*	Federalist	4. *Helped write the Declaration of Independence* First president to live in Washington
5. *Thomas Jefferson*	1801	Democratic-Republican	Author of Declaration of Independence 6. *Scientist farmer* Architect
James Madison	7. *1809*	8. *Democratic-Republican*	9. *Founder of Constitution* 10. *Husband of Dolly* 11. *Wrote 9 amendments*
12. *James Monroe*	1817	Democratic-Republican	13. *Hero of the Revolution* 14. *Monroe Doctrine*

181

6. After five minutes have elapsed, read aloud the directions for Exercise III: Part B. Then have students do this exercise. When they have completed the exercise, have them do Exercise IV. Then engage them in discussing their responses to the exercise.

STUDENT TEXT

Exercise IV

Directions: Look at the statements that follow. Check the statements that apply to you.

1. _____ I learn facts best by writing them.

2. _____ I learn facts best when I see them in lists and memorize what the lists look like.

3. _____ I learn facts best when I say them aloud.

4. _____ I learn facts best by combining 1–3.

5. _____ I have a difficult time memorizing facts, but I can remember facts when I see how they all fit together.

Introduction: Test Taking

When you put your time and effort into studying for a test, you want to do well. To do that, you need to learn the material that the test covers. You can also do better on tests if you understand how to answer the different kinds of questions. This part of the unit will suggest some tips you can use with five different types of questions:

1. true/false questions

2. multiple-choice questions

3. short-answer questions

4. matching questions

5. fact/opinion questions

---

7. Read "Introduction: Test Taking" aloud, or have a student read it to the class. Discuss briefly. Then read and discuss the material under the heading "True/False Questions." Read the directions for Exercise V aloud, or have a student read them aloud. Have the students do this exercise. Correct and discuss briefly.

STUDENT TEXT

True/False Questions

True/false questions are statements that you are asked to judge whether they are true or false?

(continued)

Tips for True/False Questions

1. Read the question carefully. If *any part* of the statement is false, then it is a false statement. Mark it false.

2. Watch for "key words" like the ones listed. Think about what these words mean in the statement; they can help you make a decision.

always	all	never
only	usually	often
frequently		

Exercise V

Directions: Read the statements that follow. Decide whether each statement is true or false. Mark a *T* for true or an *F* for false in the space after each statement.

1. All people who live in Norway have blond hair. __*F*__

2. Mercury, Venus, Jupiter, Mars, and Earth's moon are planets within our solar system. __*F*__

3. All even numbers can be divided evenly by two. __*T*__

4. Plants never grow unless they get direct sunlight. __*F*__

5. A calm always comes before a thunderstorm. __*F*__

6. Animals usually have their young in the spring. __*T*__

Multiple-Choice Questions

Multiple-choice questions ask you to choose the right answer from a group of possible answers.

Tips for Multiple-Choice Questions

1. Read the question carefully. Then see if you know the answer to the question *before* you even look at the choices.

2. Read all of the choices given, and pick the *best* answer. Some questions give two or more answers that are right in some way. You need to pick the one that is the *best* answer.

3. Be sure to read *all* of the choices given, even if the first or second one seems right. They may all be correct, and the last choice may be "all of the above."

4. If you do not know which answer is right, cross out all of the ones that you know are *wrong*. Then pick the best answer from the remaining choices. If you don't know which one is best, make a good guess.

5. You should always put down an answer on a multiple-choice question, even if it's a guess, unless your teacher tells you not to guess.

8. Follow the same procedure of reading the headings, reading the directions, and doing the exercises for Exercises VI–IX. Have students work through these exercises individually, or work them as a class. Correct the exercises together when students have finished. Discuss any questions they might have.

   When discussing facts and opinions, be sure to stress that opinions are not wrong, but to be valid they must be based on facts. Facts, however, can be wrong.

STUDENT TEXT

Exercise VI

Directions: Answer each of the questions that follow by writing the letter of the correct answer in the blank at the right.

1. The word *watch* means: ___D___

   (A) a timing device

   (B) to look at something closely

   (C) a duty on a ship

   (D) all of the above

2. Railroads played an important role in American history because ___D___

   (A) they transported all of the country's supplies

   (B) they never broke down

   (C) they were often smelly, so people started taking airplanes

   (D) they provided efficient transportation for people and supplies

3. When Columbus set sail in 1492 ___C___

   (A) the earth wasn't round

   (B) all people believed that the earth wasn't round

   (C) Columbus believed that the earth was round

   (D) almost all of the sailors believed that the earth was round

(continued)

---

4. Bats are unlike most mammals because they ___*B*___

    (A) never eat eels

    (B) have body temperature changes

    (C) cannot learn to read and write

    (D) hibernate in the summer when it is the coldest

Short-Answer Questions

Short-answer questions ask you to write in the correct answer as part of a statement. They are also called "fill-in-the-blank" questions.

Tips for Short-Answer Questions

1. Read the question carefully. Ask yourself: What is this question asking? Then write in the answer if you know it.

2. If you do not know the exact answer but do know something that is related to it, write down what you *do* know. You may get partial credit for it.

3. If you don't know the correct answer but have an idea about it, make a good guess!

Exercise VII

Directions: Read the statements that follow. Fill in the best answer you know.

1. There are _*three*_ months of the year that begin with the letter *J*.

2. The sixth American president was _*John Quincy Adams*_.

3. The three states of matter are gas, solid, and _*liquid*_.

4. The author of *The Chronicles of Narnia* is _*C.S. Lewis*_.

5. The United States is bordered by two other countries. The northern border country is _*Canada*_. The southern border country is _*Mexico*_.

Matching Questions

Matching questions usually give you two lists of information and ask you to match things on one list with things on the other.

(*continued*)

Tips for Matching Questions

1. Match the easiest things first, the ones you know most about.

2. When you have matched an item, cross out its number or letter, so you know you've already done it.

3. If you are not sure about any of the items, make a good guess!

Exercise VIII

Directions: Read the two lists below. Write the number of the piece of sports equipment in the blank before the sport for which you'd use the equipment.

a. __7__ baseball   1. shoulder pads

b. __1__ football   2. hoop

c. __2__ basketball   3. foil

d. __6__ field hockey   4. paddle

e. __4__ table tennis   5. mallet

f. __5__ polo   6. hockey stick

g. __3__ fencing   7. bat

Fact/Opinion Questions

A *fact* is a statement that can be proven to be true or false. An *opinion* is a belief. A belief cannot be proven.

Look at the question below:

The United States did not pass the Nineteenth Amendment, which gave women the right to vote, until 1920 because:

   a. men still wanted women at home to cook and raise families

   b. women were not politically wise enough

   c. in those times women were not as intelligent as men

   d. it took over forty years for enough states to pass the Nineteenth Amendment.

Although you might agree with some of the first three choices, they are really *opinions* and not *facts*. Usually true/false, multiple-choice, and short-answer questions are looking for *facts* and not *opinions*.

(continued)

Another kind of question asks you to identify statements as *fact* or *opinion*. It is important to know that opinions are not wrong. Opinions can be supported by facts.

Tips for Finding Facts

1. Facts usually explain who, what, where, or why.

2. Facts can be found in a reference book such as a dictionary, an encyclopedia, an atlas, and so on.

3. Facts are either true or false.

4. The following words are usually *not* found in factual statements.

should	maybe	could have been
if	should be	probably

Exercise IX

Directions: Read the statements that follow. Decide whether they are facts or opinions. Write an *O* after the statements that are opinions and an *F* after the statements that are facts.

1. Children should be seen and not heard. __O__

2. The United States had thirteen original states. __F__

3. Dancers have a deep appreciation for music. __O__

4. George Washington was an officer in the Continental Army. __F__

5. The United States could have been the first country in outer space if more money were given to space exploration in the 1950s. __O__

6. Abraham Lincoln walked three miles to school. __F__

7. The earth will probably have a significant climate change in the next ten years. __O__

8. All people should have a right to equal education. __O__

Additional Suggestions

1. The exercises in the first part of this unit offer students only a beginning toward gaining an understanding of their learning preferences and of the kind of environment in which they learn best. Create other activities of this kind and involve students in an ongoing experience of discovering how they learn best.

2. If you use other kinds of questions on your tests, involve students in exercises like the ones in this unit, so they can develop "testwiseness" in relation to the kinds of questions that you use.

3. Ask students to think about what questions might be on a test while they are preparing for the test. Announce a test for a specific day. Then ask students to write some questions that they think might be asked on the test. Have students hand in their questions before the test. Then give the test. After you have corrected the test and gone over it with students, discuss the questions they wrote.

4. Teach students to use this self-questioning technique as a way of studying for a test.

5. Since much of the studying for schoolwork is expected to take place at home, enlist the help of parents. Create a handout for parents such as the one at the end of this unit.

STUDENT TEXT

Unit XVI Summary

Your *study environment* can have a lot to do with how well you learn. Find out what kind of study environment works best for you. Then do your studying in that kind of environment.

When you understand how different kinds of questions work, you can often do better on tests.

1. True/false questions: If the answer is only partly false, mark it false. Watch out for "key words" like *always*, *never*, or *only*. These words can help you decide whether a statement is true or false.

2. Multiple-choice questions: Read the question, and see if you know the answer before you look at the choices. Then read all the choices, and pick the *best* answer. If you're not sure about the answer, cross out the choices that are wrong. Then choose the best remaining answer. Make a good guess!

3. Short-answer questions: Read the statement carefully. If you do not know the exact answer, write down the best answer you can think of.

4. Matching questions: Match the items you know first. Then cross them out. Make a good guess about the remaining items.

5. Fact /opinion questions: It is important to be able to tell fact from opinion. Multiple-choice questions and true/false questions are usually looking for facts and not opinions. You can recognize facts as short bits of information that you can locate in a reference book. There are also "key words" that help you decide what are not facts, such as *should be*, *probably*, and *may be*.

Suggested Retrieval Activities

As part of closure and retrieval of information learned, ask students to do one or more of the following:

- Consider the test-taking tips from this unit. Which ones are most helpful?

- Draw a picture that explains how to study for one or more of the following test-taking suggestions:

  - true/false questions

  - multiple-choice questions

  - short-answer questions

  - matching questions

  - fact/opinion questions

STUDENT TEXT

Technology Adaptation

- Create an electronic poster with study tips that work for you to share with other students in the class.

- Choose three things you have learned in this unit and post them to a class blog to share so others may learn from your findings.

- Create quizzes on sites such as www.onlinequizcreator.com. Design questions that assess your comprehension of the five different kinds of questions in this unit.

Ways You Can Help Your Child Study (for Parents)

WHERE: Your child does not need an elaborate setup. The kitchen table is a fine spot for studying. However, your child does need a spot that is fairly quiet and out of the mainstream of the family business.

WHEN: It is often best for a family to designate a certain time for studying, a time when everyone can agree to turn off the television and keep radios and CD players on low volume. For some families the hour after dinner is best. Some early risers may find the morning the most peaceful time for studying. It is probably best to avoid the times directly before bed and directly after school as these are necessary "unwinding" periods.

Whatever time your family chooses, remember that it is the repeated routine that creates a good atmosphere for studying. Also, since middle-school-age children require extra energy for their busy school days, it is helpful if an early bedtime is part of their routine.

MATERIALS: A shoebox can store rulers, pencils, pens, a small stapler, and any other items necessary for your child. It is probably a good idea if the rest of the family doesn't borrow items from this box.

Computers have become a common tool for schoolwork. Your child can use a computer for writing, research, and organization. If you have a computer at home, you'll want to be sure that your child has enough use of it for school purposes. If you do not have a computer at home, you will want to arrange for your child to use a computer at school or at a library.

Reference books, such as dictionaries, atlases, and encyclopedias, can also be kept in a special spot so they are easily available to the child. Reference books are usually available on a sign-out basis from school, so no child needs to go without materials needed for a special assignment. You can also provide these kinds of reference materials for your child by obtaining these tools in their software versions and/or gaining access to them through the Internet.

If your child's teachers require him or her to keep a notebook, check periodically to see that these notebooks are coming home and are kept updated.

Finally, ask to see your child's work. Talk about school with him or her. Discuss specific things. For instance, instead of asking how school went that day, ask: How do you like using microscopes? What are you writing about? What books are you reading? Do you find fractions difficult? What kind of governments are you learning about?

UNIT XVII
MULTIMEDIA PRESENTATIONS

STUDENT TEXT

Introduction

The use of technology makes learning a more visual and interactive process. Everyone can be creative, and the Internet and commercial software allow users the ability to do just about anything when it comes to delivering a multimedia presentation. Software standards like PowerPoint and Internet presentation tools like Prezi and PowToon allow you to make things fun while giving information at the same time. For enhanced video-heavy presentations, try Animoto and MovieMaker, or create a channel on websites like Vimeo. Still yet, photos may be manipulated using commercial products like Photoshop while free applications like PicMonkey do similar things in just a few clicks—and without cost to the user.

Multimedia presentations using electronic delivery methods allow users to share information in interesting formats. Further, it allows you to be creative and engaged. Traditional presentation resources only allowed users to present words and pictures, information given in silos rather than blended together. Now you have the ability to make a fully interactive presentation, complete with text and information, photos, videos, and graphics. Presentations may be shared with the intended audience, or presentations may be shared via the Internet and distributed to virtually any audience.

Suggested Directions for Unit XVII

The following contains a list of suggested directions for Unit XVII. Using the first step as a base, the steps that follow number one increase in complexity to deliver a comprehensive project at the conclusion if all steps are followed. Teachers may elect to add and/or delete steps from the list or include other multimedia presentation formats and requirements to enhance the finished product.

Step 1: During a class session, briefly demonstrate to students what a presentation should contain (adapt to fit a current class lesson, for example). Have students explore different commercial presentation software and presentation applications using the web. Then, allow students to choose from a list of topics related to the given lesson and prepare their own original presentation. These presentations should be simple; information-only presentations ensure students understand how to capture their message and use their chosen platform.

Step 2: Using the same presentation previously prepared, have students incorporate at least three pictures or graphics to enhance their presentation. The pictures/graphics should be modified for effect using one of the example programs listed, or students may choose to use a different product with teacher approval. The pictures/graphics should enhance the project and provide focus and clarity to the intended audience.

Step 3: Using the same presentation previously prepared, have students incorporate at least a two-minute motion-picture segment. Students may choose two to four movie clips to support their topic and include at least two minutes of video into their presentation. If video camera equipment is available to students, they may choose to make their own movie for incorporation into the presentation. Students may choose to use presentation software available on the school computers, or use free web-based applications. Suggest students format the presentation to enhance it by showing a process, being persuasive like a movie trailer, or being informational.

Step 4: Have students present their multimedia presentations to the class. This can be achieved by simply presenting the multimedia presentation, or having students or create a channel on websites like Vimeo. Have the audience provide input about what worked in the other presentations and what needed improvements.

Step 5: Assign students to do a presentation about a product. Students will have flexibility in choosing the product they want to research and present to the class. Students will use all of the available methods known to create and use multimedia presentations (available software, still pictures, motion pictures, etc.). Give students guidelines on what to include, what not to include, and how it should be formatted/structured, so a project grade can be assessed. It is suggested to use the exercise after the class has completed the "Organizing Ideas" unit since that work complements this exercise.

Additional Suggestions

In order to familiarize students with a variety of technological resources, ask individual students to select a resource, research what it can do, and provide a demonstration to the class.

Animoto: an online service that helps create videos from images and video clips.

Blabberize: animate images and make them talk.

Blogspot: allows users to create a simple blog.

Diigo: an online bookmarking service that supports students as they work on a research project.

Edmodo: a resource that provides a way to share classroom content in a way similar to Twitter.

Educreations: tool for sharing video lessons.

GIMP: free photo editing program

Gliffy: collaborative tool for designing flowcharts and diagrams.

Glogster: an online web service that helps create virtual posters through the use of multimedia.

Google Docs: a word-processing resource to facilitate sharing, creating, and editing documents.

Google Plus: facilitates the use of video chats.

iMovie: video editing software free on Apple computers.

LucidChart: create online diagrams and flow charts.

MyFakeWall: fake Facebook-style profiles for historical figures.

Photovisi: photo collages for downloading and printing.

PicMonkey: photo editing.

Plurk: a social network similar to Twitter.

PowToon: create animated videos and presentations.

Prezi: cloud-based presentation and storytelling tool for presenting ideas on a virtual canvas.

ProConLists: an electronic listing of positives and negatives of an issue.

Queeky: an online drawing tool.

ReadWriteThink: creates cartoons with images and thought bubbles.

Rubistar: an online tool to help design scoring rubrics.

Schoology: a website designed to manage lessons, engage students, and share content.

Shape Collage: facilitates in making an electronic collage.

StudyBlue: online flash cards, quizzes, and study guides for sharing.

Survey Monkey: creates a survey and analyzes the results.

TeacherTube: a video-sharing website designed specifically for classroom use.

Tumblr: an easy tool for blogging.

Twitter: an easy-to-use microblog.

Vimeo: video-sharing website on which users can upload, share, and view videos.

Wall Wisher (padlet): creates a multimedia wall for students to brainstorm ideas, notes, etc.

Webquest: facilitates students as they research content online.

Weebly: a tool for creating a website.

Windows Movie Maker: video editing software free on Windows computers.

Wordle: a resource that generates word clouds from text.

YouTube: video-sharing website on which users can upload, share, and view videos

---

STUDENT TEXT

Step 1: Explore different commercial presentation software and presentation applications using the web. Choose from a list of topics related to the given lesson and prepare an original presentation.

Step 2: Using the same presentation previously prepared, incorporate at least three pictures or graphics to enhance the presentation. The pictures/graphics should be modified for effect using one of the example programs listed, or you may choose to use a different product with teacher approval. The pictures/graphics should enhance the project and provide focus and clarity to the intended audience.

Step 3: Using the same presentation previously prepared, incorporate at least a two-minute motion-picture segment. Choose two to four movie clips to support the topic and include at least two minutes of video in their presentation. If video camera equipment is available, make a movie for incorporation into the presentation. Choose presentation software available on the school computers, or use free web-based applications. Format the presentation to enhance it by showing a process, being persuasive like a movie trailer, or being informational.

Step 4: Present the multimedia presentations to the class. This can be accomplished by using a multimedia presentation, or by creating a channel on websites like Vimeo.

Step 5: Do a presentation about a product. Use all of the available methods known to create and use multimedia presentations (available software, still pictures, motion pictures, etc.).

Select one or more resources from the listing that follows. Research what it can do, and provide a demonstration to the class.

Unit XVII Summary

Using a variety of electronic resources is a twenty-first-century skill for both teachers and students. Students must be prepared to learn with multimedia as well as be able to demonstrate learning through the same.

Most professions use electronic resources for sharing information, receiving information, or learning. Journalism, engineering, medicine, education, entertainment, and a variety of other commercial industries all use multimedia to produce, advertise, and sell products and services. The challenge for students and educators is not necessarily learning and knowing how to use these resources; rather, the challenge will be to stay up to date with what is available, most useful, and trending.

Suggested Retrieval Activities

As part of closure and retrieval of information learned, ask students to do one or more of the following:

- Partner with school clubs/organizations who may be conducting a fund-raiser. Offer to have students prepare a presentation for them to advertise their product (like students did in the final exercise of this unit). This allows for students to practice their multimedia presentation skills by developing a useable product for themselves and others.

- Have students research other multimedia presentation tools online covered in this unit: software/programs, websites, picture editing, moviemaking tools, and so on. Then have students create an alternative presentation for content covered later in class.

- Students could vary the previous activity and present to others how to use the multimedia presentation software/website by performing an in-class demonstration.

STUDENT TEXT

Technology Adaptation

N/A

UNIT XVIII
Posttest

Suggested Directions for the Study Skills Posttest

1. Explain to students that the purpose of the posttest is to measure what has been learned from using *The hm Learning and Study Skills Program: Level I.*

2. In addition to marking "Always," "Sometimes," or "Never," students should include an explanation as to why there might be a difference between what they actually do and what they should be doing.

STUDENT TEXT

Directions for the Study Skills Posttest

After completing the units in this program, what have you learned and what habits have you modified? Please complete the survey that follows and explain the benefit of each study habit. Compare this survery to the one you completed at the beginning of the program.

Study Skills Survey

	Always	Sometimes	Never
I review my assignments every day. *The more frequent the review of daily lessons, the easier it is to recall the information on test day. Frequent review supports long-term retention.*			
I try to study in a quiet place. *Although some students believe they can do several things at one time, this is not true for learning. The human brain can only concentrate on one thing at a time.*			
When necessary, I ask for help. *Students need to use the resources available to them. This can be parents, classmates, or teachers.*			
I keep a folder for each subject. *A key to staying organized is making sure that each subject has its own folder and place to keep handouts and assignments.*			
I keep my folders organized. *Middle school students are notorious for not keeping folders organized. However, they usually respond positively to reminders.*			
I write sample test questions and answer the questions. *Part of preparing for an exam is anticipating what might be asked. Students should get in the habit of writing sample test questions and answers as part of the reviewing process.*			
I do my homework as early in the day as possible. *Students are busy people, too. If they wait too long after school to begin completing homework, it will not be good. The later in the evening, the more tired the student becomes. The more tired the student, the less productive in terms of learning.*			
I keep a "to-do" list of assignments. *A good habit to develop at an early age is keeping a "to-do" list. For students this would include homework assignments, due dates, extracurricular schedules, etc.*			
I turn in all assignments on time. *Procrastination works against most people. Most teachers are unwilling to give full credit to students that turn in assignments late. Students should understand it is foolish to lose points because of tardiness.*			
When I take notes, I always write a summary from my notes of what I learned. *Reviewing and writing a summary of notes taken from a book, a class discussion, or a class lecture helps to cement the information into long-term memory.*			
I begin studying for tests several days in advance of the exam. *Last-minute test preparation is not a good habit. Learning in small increments is much more efficient, and it also helps to eliminate test anxiety.*			

	Always	Sometimes	Never
I compare my notes to a classmate's notes. *Comparing notes with a classmate can help both students. It can ensure that notes are complete and comprehensive.*			
I take written notes over text material. *When a reading assignment is made, students should assume the teacher believes the information is important enough to warrant note taking. This usually means the information will appear on an upcoming test.*			
I look at bold print, italics, the writing in margins, and study questions before I begin a reading assignment. *Using the features of a text is a good studying strategy. The author and publisher usually designate what is the most important content to be learned.*			
I ask the teacher to explain things when I'm confused. *It is surprising how few students will stop a teacher and ask for further explanation. This may be a fear of believing he or she is the only one that is unsure. Regardless, students should be encouraged to ask when something is unclear.*			
When learning new information, I read the text slowly. *Good readers know that different tasks require different rates of reading. As a result, adjustments to reading rates should be made depending on familiarity of content and purpose for reading.*			
When I have several homework assignments, I finish the hardest ones first. *There is a feeling of satisfaction when a difficult task is completed. If the more challenging assignment is "saved for later," fatigue sets in and it makes it even more difficult to complete.*			
When I sit down to study, I have all my supplies organized and ready to use— paper, pencils, computer, etc. *Organization is important, and students should designate a specific place for studying each day. Students can waste several minutes of a studying time by repeatedly trying to find supplies.*			